I HEAR THE BUGLE'S CALL

A young boy's journey through the Civil War

by Dan Makarewich

Copyright 2014 by Dan Makarewich

All rights reserved. No part of this book may be reproduced or transmitted in any form or by any means, electronic or mechanical, including photocopying, recording, or by any information storage and retrieval system, without permission in writing from the publisher.

Published by Dan Makarewich, 7530 Willis Road, Ypsilanti, MI 48197. Telephone 734-487-5829. E-mail: danielmakarewich@yahoo.com

Publisher's Cataloging-in-Publication Data
Mararewich, Dan
   I hear the bugle's call/Dan Makarewich
     Ypsilanti, Mich.
               p.   cm.   ill.
     ISBN 978-1-4951-2681-9
     1. History–United States.

PROJECT COORDINATION BY BOOKABILITY OF MICHIGAN LLC

Printed in Canada

Dedication

To my wife, Barb, with whom I have had the pleasure of traveling our life's journey, and to the memory of all the soldiers, young and old, who long ago heard the bugle's call.

Beat! beat! drums!—blow! bugles! Blow!

Through the windows—through doors—burst like a ruthless force,

Into the solemn church, and scatter the congregation,

Into the school where the scholar is studying;

Leave not the bridegroom quiet—no happiness must he have—now with his bride,

Nor the peaceful farmer any peace, ploughing his field or gathering his grain,

So fierce you whirr and pound you drums—so shrill your bugles blow.

Walt Whitman, *Drum Taps*

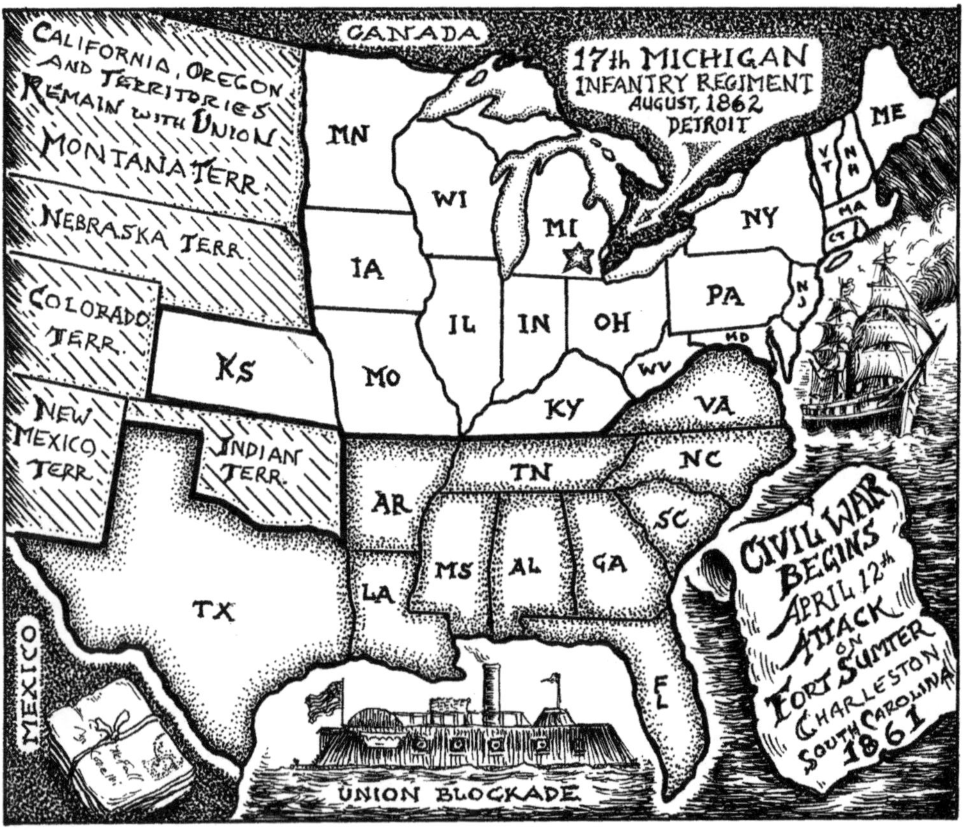
CANADA
CALIFORNIA, OREGON AND TERRITORIES REMAIN WITH UNION
MONTANA TERR.
NEBRASKA TERR.
COLORADO TERR.
NEW MEXICO TERR.
INDIAN TERR.
17th MICHIGAN INFANTRY REGIMENT AUGUST, 1862 DETROIT
MN
WI
MI
IA
IL
IN
OH
PA
NY
ME
VT
NH
MA
CT
NJ
MD
KS
MO
KY
WV
VA
NC
TN
AR
SC
MS
AL
GA
LA
TX
FL
MEXICO
UNION BLOCKADE
CIVIL WAR BEGINS APRIL 12th ATTACK ON FORT SUMTER CHARLESTON SOUTH CAROLINA 1861

Prologue

My first recollection of American Civil War History was when I read *Rifles for Watie*, by Harold Keith—A Newberry Medal winner. This exciting story of a young boy joining the Union Army and experiencing the scenes of battle caused me to read it multiple times as a young student. I certainly had no inclination that one day long into the future I would write a story of another young boy engulfed in that same war.

This story chronicles a family's civil war experience using the genre of historical fiction. The journey is told by Jacob Britt who, as a living descendent of the McFall brothers, is taken back to experience the war in all its brutality, intensity and gallantry.

Though I am not a member of the McFall family, I became interested in their ancestors' experiences during the war. Their lives became known as I researched the volunteer regiment and company to which three of the brothers belonged. I benefitted greatly by the information provided by McFall descendants. Learning about the family's pre-war history gave me a better understanding of the men's later lives.

As I continued my research, I discovered much in the way of primary sources such as military records, deeds, obituaries and other documents. But the sources that would bring these men to life—diaries, journals, letters were not to be found. Fortunately, I did discover letters written by other soldiers who served with the McFalls and shared common experiences. From these letters I was able to understand a great deal about what the brothers confronted starting on their first day in uniform, and until the day the war ended for them.

I have attempted to recreate the lives of the McFalls by composing letters they might have written home to family and friends. I have also composed letters describing the feelings of the people back home.

Please keep in mind that the letters you read were only the ones that the McFall family exchanged and kept in their possession. Also, it was common at the time to use the abbreviation ult. for ultimate (occurring in the month proceeding the present) and inst. for instant (the present or current month) when referring to letters received.

Most of the people you will meet were actual members of the McFall family, or their comrades. Others are fictitious, but do express realistic feelings of people at home conducting their lives as best they could.

As I continued my research, I became enthralled by the life and death experiences of the McFall family as their participation in the war intensified.

The events that whirled around them, the actions they took that would result in personal glory and tragedy as well, is a quintessential story of the Civil War.

It is my hope the reader will agree.

Daniel Makarewich
Summer, 2014

The Journey Begins

The narrow wooden stairs leading to the attic emitted a somewhat eerie groan as I slowly ascended them gripping my scout flashlight. I wasn't sure what I would find on my self-initiated adventure. I was told by my Great Aunt Mildred that she thought there was an old "Saratoga" trunk in the attic that I might find interesting though she couldn't recall the last time she had looked through it. As I opened the door, I saw a string overhead that connected to a light bulb, which when pulled, illuminated the attic with a dim, dusty glow. I slowly walked around looking for the family trunk. After a few minutes of searching I came across what appeared to be the object of my search.

What brought me on this adventure was an American History class assignment to investigate my family's story. My Grandpa Norm had told me stories of the McFall side of the family, especially the nineteenth-century stories of Cornelius and Catherine McFall and their children. I had heard family tales of the McFall's moving from New York along the Erie Canal and then coming to Michigan by steamboat during its first year of statehood.

What really peaked my interest were the tales of the McFall brothers and the Civil War. Grandpa Norm had mentioned stories that were passed down from his father, Floyd McFall, of the four brothers who lived during the Civil War years and the three who lived into the twentieth-century.

I had seen the gravesites of two brothers—their headstones engraved with the inscription: "Co E 17th Michigan Volunteer Regiment." And on one of the gravestones, Daniel McFall's, the additional inscription of "Medal of Honor."

For years I had heard numerous family stories about this part of their history, but the personal connection was missing due to the lack of any letters, diaries or journals left by these ancestors. But there still remained a legend that there may yet be letters somewhere in the attic.

As I opened the dusty chest, I saw an old gray, wool blanket and underneath the blanket was something wrapped in a cotton pillowcase. As I looked into the pillowcase, I found a cane and pulled it out. My eyes were drawn to the carving encircling the cane. It was a serpent stopped in motion.

I Hear the Bugle's Call

I shined my flashlight closer and noticed the top of the handle. "Schuyler McFall" was carved into what appeared to be a bone. With this discovery my heart and mind felt like they were racing in competition with each other. I set the cane aside hoping that I may have found my family's treasure of all treasures and excitedly continued the inspection of the trunk.

I burrowed through other objects such as old photographs of unknown people in old fashion clothes. At the bottom of the trunk I came across a large folder. This folder had a thick piece of twine wrapped around it and knotted to hold in its bulging contents. I examined my discovery and came across the words "War Letters" written on the cover. My eyes widened and again my heart began to beat faster. I quickly cut open the twine with my Scout knife. The folder erupted with small bundles of faded envelopes, containing letters. Each bundle was tied with yarn or a ribbon. I held them closer to the flashlight. Each bundle had a date written on the top of the envelope such as August 1862 or January 1863. I knew I had to open these now. My curiosity was as intense as my heart rate.

I sank into an old oak rocking chair. With the dim light of the attic bulb and my flashlight I opened the first bundle marked August 1862.

Thus began an incredible adventure, the adventure of a lifetime. I soon found myself on a journey back in time where I experienced the whirlwind called the Civil War. For me the stories of my McFall ancestors became reality—the sights and sounds of battle all too real. Looking back today as an adult I can still recall my journey as that young boy. Once again, "I hear the bugle's call."

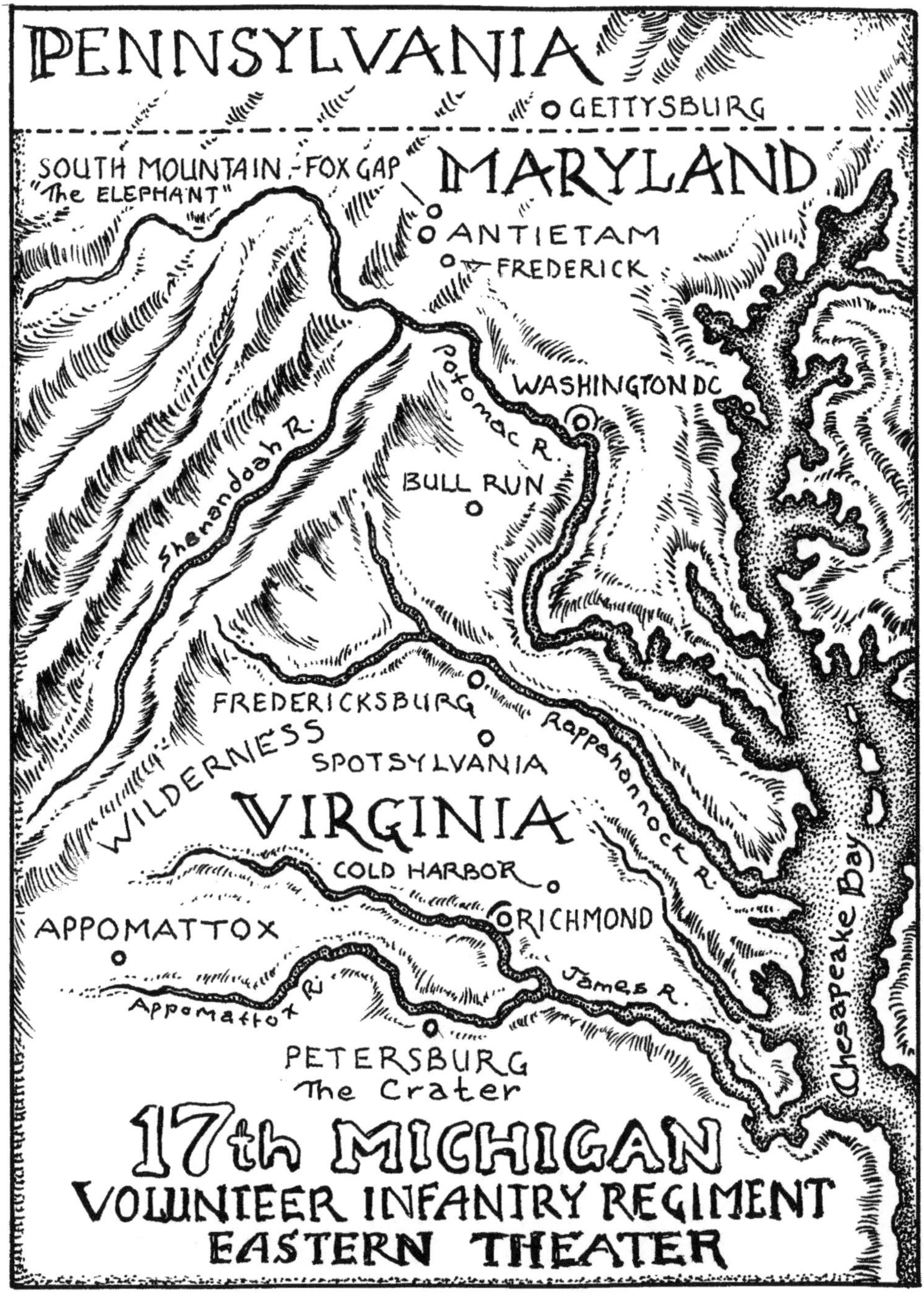
PENNSYLVANIA
GETTYSBURG
MARYLAND
SOUTH MOUNTAIN - FOX GAP
"The ELEPHANT"
ANTIETAM
FREDERICK
Potomac R.
WASHINGTON DC
Shenandoah R.
BULL RUN
FREDERICKSBURG
Rappahannock R.
WILDERNESS
SPOTSYLVANIA
VIRGINIA
COLD HARBOR
RICHMOND
APPOMATTOX
James R.
Appomattox R.
PETERSBURG
The Crater
Chesapeake Bay
17th MICHIGAN
VOLUNTEER INFANTRY REGIMENT
EASTERN THEATER

BULLY 17TH!

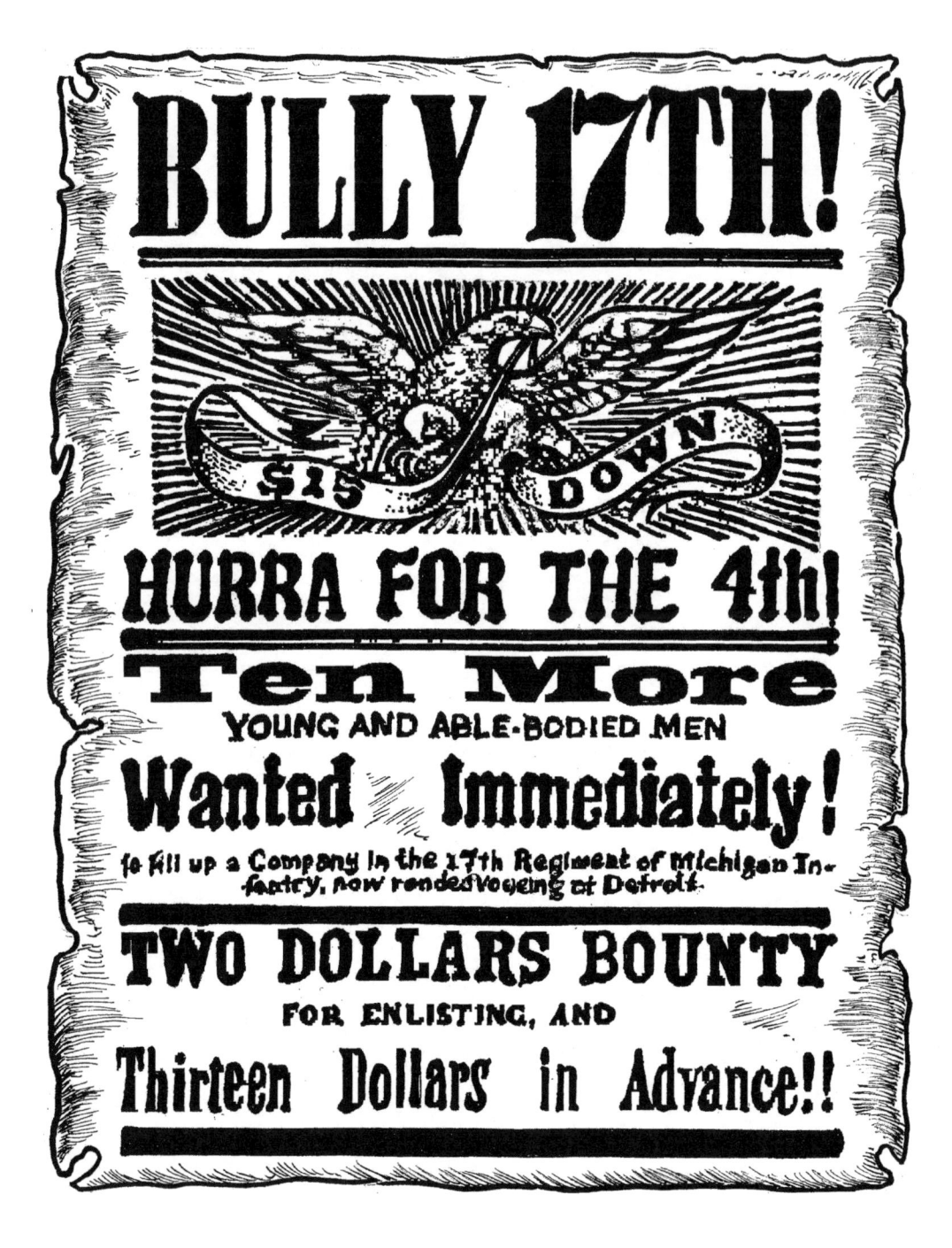

$15 DOWN

HURRA FOR THE 4th!

Ten More
YOUNG AND ABLE-BODIED MEN

Wanted Immediately!

to fill up a Company in the 17th Regiment of Michigan Infantry, now rendezvousing at Detroit.

TWO DOLLARS BOUNTY
FOR ENLISTING, AND

Thirteen Dollars in Advance!!

"Brothers in Arms"
August, 1862

I held the first bundle of letters in my lap and cut the yarn holding them. I removed two folded pages from an envelope dated "August 1862." It was addressed to Mr. and Mrs. Cornelius McFall, Cone, Michigan. I eagerly began to read its contents.

> Detroit Barracks
> Friday, August 22, 1862

Our Dear Parents,

I am writing this for myself and for Harrison. We thought one letter could say the same as two. While I am writing to you Schuyler is writing to Lomira. I know everyone is very anxious to get news from us. We are well and having a grand time. We are two miles or so from the depot where we arrived at about 10 o'clock yesterday morning. By the time we marched over to the barracks we were plenty tired and hungry. But the victuals we were given was not fit for man nor beast. We had the good fortune to come across some old vendors selling pies and fruit. The pies were first rate. Some of the men ate too many sweet foods, and found themselves ailing.

Let me tell you about our mustering in at Ypsilanti. After you folks left us in town, Schulyer, Harrison and I saw a sign that told us to walk over to a wagon shop owned by Mr. Thompson. He allowed all of us to bunk on the top two floors. At Hewitt Hall near the depot there was a meeting where we elected our officers. Gabriel Campbell is our Captain.

A sword and sash was presented to Captain Campbell by Professor Sill from the Normal School. We were told that the people of Ypsilanti raised the money for them. Ladies representing some of the churches in town presented each of us with a Bible and a housewife—with thread, needles, buttons and such. You know, Ma, I think me and Schuyler can handle such a kit but I'm not sure of Harrison.

I Hear the Bugle's Call

The next day we took the cars for Detroit. As we pulled out of the station we agreed that we were excited to start this trip though we don't know when we'll be back. You know we enlisted to restore our Union for which some good men have already paid the price. With the Lord's help we'll see it done.

It's now the afternoon and we've just been issued our equipment. Here's what we get—two shirts, one pair of light blue pants, one light blue overcoat, one dark blue fatigue coat, one dark blue dress coat, white cotton gloves, two pairs flannel drawers, two pairs of socks, one pair of shoes, one fatigue cap, one hat with black plume fastened up on one side with an eagle plate, a blue cord and tassels—bugle in front, knapsack, haversack, cartridge belt, canteen, and Austrian rifle. When we put this all together it's like carrying a store on our back.

We'll send money home when we get paid. We don't know when that will be. I have to end this letter.

> Your loving sons,
> Daniel and Harrison
> Company E
> 17th Michigan Infantry

Although the writing was hard to read at times I was able to make sense of most of the words. I came to the end and I read the names Daniel and Harrison. I thought to myself, could these be two of the McFall brothers from family legend? I felt that I just discovered a real family treasure!

Should I search out my family downstairs and present my find or stay and read on? My curiosity won out and I continued to read the remaining letters in this first packet.

Detroit Barracks
Friday, August 22, 1862

My Dear Lomira,

I wanted to write you as soon as I had time knowing you'd be anxious about us. We brothers are here at the barracks about two miles from the depot. We arrived from Ypsilanti at about 10 o'clock yesterday and marched to camp. When we got here we was plenty tired and hungry. They gave us some awful smelling beef and biscuits. We had better luck eating when we bought some pies and fruit from some vendors. Let me tell you what's happened since we bid farewell. After you and the family left us me and Harrison and Daniel saw a sign that said "Company E report to Thompson's Wagon Shop." The wagon shop was across from the depot. This was the place our company would stay. Men bunked on the 2nd and 3rd floors.

In the evening we all walked over to Hewitt Hall across the street for a meeting. At the meeting we elected Gabriel Campbell from Augusta to be our Captain. A professor Sill from the Normal School presented him with a fine looking sword and sash. There had been a collection in town to raise the money for this. All of us were presented with a Bible from the city churches and also what is called a housewife. Daniel and I were kidding Harrison not to injure hisself before we see the rebels. There's a rumor that we'll be leaving for Washington soon. I got to stop now for there's a call to form up. I'll write again soon. Hug the children for me, tell them papa is thinking of them.

Your loving husband, Schuyler

Fort Baker
Washington City
Sunday, August 31, 1862

Dear Ma and Pa,

Well we finally got to Washington City. Daniel said it was my turn to write so here's what we've been up to. Last Sunday, while we were still back in Detroit we joined a few other men and went over to the 4th Michigan Cavalry camp

I Hear the Bugle's Call

for a Sabbath Service. A good sermon was led by a Chaplain with the unit. After the service some of the boys walked over to Elmwood Cemetery.

On Monday we got paid. We received our $25 government bonus and our first month's pay of $13. Daniel and I are sending you our bonus pay to keep for us. Look in the folded envelope inside this one.

On Wednesday we were formed up and marched downtown to honor Colonel Orlando Willcox. He was captured at the Bull Run Battle and recently exchanged. He looks to be a good man to lead us. He told us that men from Michigan will be part of a strong fighting army. And although we may not know each other now we are comrades in arms. That night we boarded the *May Queen* for our trip East. Most of us had never seen a steamboat up close so riding one would be an adventure for sure. On board we were fed hard crackers and some kind of meat. They said it was beef but we aint so sure. The ride went well and about sunrise the next morning we got to Cleveland. At Cleveland we boarded the cars heading toward Pittsburgh. We arrived at Pittsburgh around 7 o'clock in the evening and got a fine supper provided by the ladies of the city. By that time we was plenty hungry too. The people treated us like heroes. Schuyler joked that if this is gonna be our reception in the war, we like this kind of fighting.

The scenery in Pennsylvania was first rate. We saw some very good cropland and well kept barns. A ways off we could see mountains and valleys. Pa, the corn and wheat along the way look a little better than ours. Maybe more rain here.

On Friday the 29th we arrived at Harrisburg, but were not fed as well as in Pittsburgh. We only stayed a short while and arrived in Baltimore later than day. We had to march aways to another depot and we sang "Battle Cry of Freedom" while we marched. We didn't know many of the words, but the boys from the Normal School did and happily taught us. I must say we sounded as good as the church choir. After sundown we was crowded into cattle cars and off to Washington.

We arrived in Washington City about daylight, and were led to a campground near the Capitol where we were fed a breakfast of more meat–and bread and coffee. We could see the Capitol Building. They are still working on the domed top of the building. We then got orders to march to a Fort Baker. With no tents we spent the night in a cold rainfall.

Today, Sunday, tents arrived and we can begin to dry out. The job for our company is to guard a bridge over the East branch of the Potomac River. They call it the Navy Yard Bridge. We also have been doing a lot of drilling, learning different formations for battle. In fact we spend most of our day either at drill or having inspections. Schuyler, Daniel and me have been sharing the same tent. Its big enough for a couple of more but for now just us are in it. Also, we've been taking turns helping with the cooking. Schuyler has become our main cook, but Daniel and I are handy at it too. We bought newspapers today to find out what's going on. We also went down to the river to bathe for the first time since we left. We would sure like to read some hometown papers. Here is also a list of things we would be grateful to receive from home--two or three pairs of socks, pencils and writing paper, envelopes, stamps (we can mail home letters free but stamps might make the mail go faster), and any homemade treats like Ma's cooking or Lomira's apple cake. Mrs. E. M. Foote in Ypsilanti is organizing packages for our company. Send things to her and tell her who we are.

I'm going to end this long letter now. You and others can see our address so please write us soon. For myself and for Daniel.

> Your loving son,
> Harrison
> Company E
> 17th Michigan
> Washington

I Hear the Bugle's Call

Cone, Michigan
September 7, 1862

Dear Sons, Daniel and Harrison,

Your Pa and I received yours letters of August 22 and 31. We are relieved that all of you are in good health. We were very anxious to hear from you boys while reading war news and hearing rumors—some good and some bad. We and Lomira have a plan about writing. She'll write to Schuyler of course and tell us what he says while we write to you boys and tell her anything she hasn't heard.

We received the money you sent. We'll keep it safe. We're going to put together the essentials you asked for and John and Emma will add a few treasures of their own. I'm sure I can rustle up a batch of cookies and perhaps some dried fruit now that it's coming on to harvest time. I have written to Mrs. Foote in Ypsilanti. She has agreed to add our package to the others she is sending to your company.

Daniel, John tells us your corn is looking just fine and a second crop of hay on the east 10 acres is about ready to cut. Pa had John and Thomas cleaning the ditch bank behind our barn. They have a plan to cut some cords of wood at your place toward the back near the fence line and ours this fall. They hope to get at least 20-30 cords. If we do we might be able to sell the extra in town.

Some of the ladies in church have begun a sewing circle. They are making socks, shirts and other clothes that might come in handy when the weather turns cold. I and Emma have been helping when we can. We'll be sending these off to you boys as soon as we can finish them.

I must confess I do worry a lot about you boys. Pa says "the boys can take care of themselves" but I know he's worried for you too. We know you're good boys and are looking out for us and our country, and doing us proud.

John keeps busy looking after your farm and looking in on Schuyler's from time to time. Tell Harrison, Katie Welch has asked how he's doing. She says she would look forward to receiving a letter from him if he has the time. Katie's a good Christian girl from good parents. Harrison, you write her now when you get the chance.

I'll finish and pray you boys are home soon. Daniel, you and Schuyler look out for your little brother and Harrison you mind them now.

Your loving parents

Paint Creek
September 6, 1862

My Dearest Husband,

I was quite relieved to receive your first letter since you and your brothers left us. Though it's only been a few weeks it seems like months since we were together. I and the children are holding up well. They ask about you and I tell them Papa has gone on a trip with Uncle Harrison and Uncle Daniel and will be back soon.

I've been working at night with them on a little schooling. Elenora is working on her handwriting and reading. I've been reading nursery rhymes to them. They question me about what is Papa doing? I tell them he's on a long trip.

Thomas and Samantha have been a great help on the farm. Thomas and John have plans to cut some wood down by the creek before winter and hope to sell some. I do pray you'll be home safe here before we see the next winter.

Elenora has been helping with some of the farm chores. She's been helping me fetch in the eggs from the coop and feeding the dogs and cats. She's even helping watch Preston for me while I'm busy.

The weather continues to be hot and dry but the apples and peaches are coming on. Though I hope to start putting up preserves for winter soon.

Pastor Hoover stopped by during the week to see how we are coming along. He said he received a letter from Daniel recently. I'll be sending you some baked goods and your favorite pipe tobacco plus some of the newspapers. Also I'll send along some writing paper and stamps. Please write as often as you can. I do worry greatly about you and your brothers. Everyone here at home are proud of what you boys are doing for our country.

I Hear the Bugle's Call

I must end now and put the babes to sleep. Next time I write you I might have a surprise to tell you.

Until then my love,

Lomira

Saturday, September 6, 1862

Dear Daniel and Brothers

I pray this letter finds all of you safe from danger and in good health. Daniel, I received yours of the 31st ult. and was much pleased in reading it. I have been kept informed by John and by Lomira on the early weeks of your travels. Be assured that everyone here are might proud of what you boys are doing for us and our great nation.

The women of the church led by Mrs. Tyler and Mrs. Childs have organized a sewing circle. They said that with winter approaching they wanted to make sure you and the other men of your company have plenty of warm socks and an extra blanket. We do hope you won't be needing them cause with God's help this war will soon be over.

I'm pleased to hear that your company have many good Christian men and the evils of drink won't slow their mission to do God's work.

Each Sabbath I am pleased to see your families attending the sermon and we together with our neighbors pray for the safe and speedy return of all our men. Please write when you find time.

In God's Name

Pastor Neal Hoover
First Congregational Church
and Society of Augusta

After reading these letters I was overwhelmed. I wasn't sure exactly what everything in the letters meant, but I was sure I was on to something.

A strange sensation came over me as I put the letters aside. I closed my eyes for what I thought was but a few seconds, but then when I opened them I was being spoken to by a man in a blue uniform.

Well boys its good to finally hear from our folks back home. And by the way Harrison, whats this I hear about Katie Welch askin about you? Now, why would an educated young girl want to be knowing about a farm boy from Cone? Well Schuyler, she must have heard I was one of those brave soldiers who signed up to march forward and whip Secession! Now don't that sound like recruitin poster talk, Daniel?

These two soldiers turned to me and I suddenly realized that I had become Daniel McFall, the third part of our family legend. By some strange phenomenon I had become a soldier in the Union Army. I quickly responded, "I agree completely Schuyler." I then looked around and saw that I and my newly recognized family were sitting on a blanket in a canvas tent filled with the smell of a cooking fire from outside and damp clothes inside. To add to my confusion it become evident to me I had gained the knowledge and personality of Daniel McFall, the middle brother of the older Schuyler and the youngest brother Harrison. We walked outside the tent to sit around a cooking fire where some coffee was near boil and the smell of some kind of stew was escaping from a sheet tin boiler. Harrison opened up a haversack and pulled out some biscuits that were near rock hard but when soaked in the coffee would become edible. Four other soldiers joined us. I found later they were James Masters, Michael Breining and the Hardy brothers. All from Paint Creek.

After finishing our meal and cleaning up Sergeant Maltman came over and said "I want Masters and you McFall boys to fall in for guard duty at the bridge in thirty minutes.

A damp north wind was blowing. We put out our cooking fire and collected up our cartridge belts, canteens and muskets and with a few more from our company marched out to the Navy Bridge which stretched across the Potomac River into Virginia. Our orders were to let no one cross either way without a written pass. We were told Washington was full of rebel spies and Yankee deserters. We all stood guard at the east post side of the bridge.

We spend four hours stopping men on horseback and driving wagons checking their passes. We did find one young Yankee deserter hiding under some baskets in a wagon going south. He was a scared looking soldier that looked younger than Harrison. We rousted him up and turned him over to the Provost Guard. I felt sorry for him and hoped he'd get fair treatment.

We came off guard duty, but we hardly had time to catch a short meal of coffee, beans and biscuits before we heard what I later learned was the bugle call for the regiment to form up. At the formation we were told of the afternoon routine by our Captain Campbell. We then were marched out to a field north of our camp. There for the first time I witnessed what I had become part of. In this field I saw many hundreds of men in formations led by officers standing or on horseback barking out orders that seem incomprehensible.

Our regiment began to drill. I later learned these tactics were called marching by column and deploying into line. I must say I was amazed that as Daniel, I seemed to catch on to these drills rather well rather well.

Finally around 3 o'clock we were formed up into a brigade formation. Here we stood with three other regiments for a review by our brigade commander Colonel Orlando Willcox and his staff. We stood at attention with our regimental flags fluttering in the wind. I do think we gave a good impression. As I looked around next to my newly discovered brothers I truly felt a part of this army.

It was early September and there were rumors that General Robert E. Lee and the Confederate Army was moving north. Our regiment had been issued ammunition, food and other supplies which had to mean we will soon be on the march. I had become rather good with the rifle musket after some rough trials getting use to such a weapon.

We had become fairly efficient at cooking for ourselves and I'm learning more about them and the McFall family back home. I listened carefully when Harrison read me the letter home he had written as he wrote it from both of us. By talking with my brothers I learned more about Daniel and why he was here. I didn't know where this strange series of events would lead me but I started to think I was up to it. We were truly brothers-in-arms.

After one rather busy and tiring day we heard tattoo sounding and lights out. As I lay on my blanket I began to feel that I'd be confronting new and unknown challenges soon. I hoped I, Daniel McFall, would be ready. Then sleep overcame my thoughts.

I Hear the Bugle's Call

I've Seen the Elephant!
September – October 1862

I awoke and found myself back in the attic sitting in the rocking chair. What had just happened? I looked around and found myself alone with the packets of letters all about.

I felt as if I'd just been the main character in some war inspired video game. I felt strange, not fearful or confused, but excited. I decided to continue reading the letters. I wasn't at all sure what happened or why, but my curiosity led me further. My thought was that after I finished the letters, I could go downstairs and share my discoveries with my family. The big question would be would they believe my story. But perhaps the bigger question—would I believe it? I picked up the next packet of letters dated September, 1862.

The first letter was addressed to Harrison from a name that wasn't familiar. A girl by the name Katie Welch.

Wednesday, September 10, 1862

Dear Harrison,

I thank you for yours of August 31st ult. I trust this letter finds you and your brothers safe. We have heard of your regiment's travel to Washington. Some of the soldiers in the 17th have written home and we read of your travel in the newspaper. It sure sounds exciting to travel that distance by train and look over the scenery. Though I suspect the reason for your travel could be more pleasant.

Back here in Cone life goes on as usual. Except when it comes to my new position. Being the new teacher has its interesting times. My class is made up of fifteen students, but with harvesting going on I don't expect to see all of them till later in the fall. Until more students arrive I have been teaching five to ten of the younger ones. We spend time on learning their ABC's and simple arithmetic. Each morning as I look at the flag I think of you and your brothers and others who are standing tall for our flag and country. I'm giving my best effort in teaching at Cone School.

My family is doing well and Papa says our crops should bring in a good penny or two this fall. You asked in your letter about a picture of me. I must confess I don't have a recent one (a picture of me at five years old wouldn't do) but we may have our school picture taken at school by a traveling photographer from Monroe. Perhaps I then can honor your request.

I will end now as I must plan the children's lessons for tomorrow.

I pray for your safety and for the cause you are fighting for.

Sincerely,

Katie Welch
Cone, Michigan

As I finished this letter it became apparent to me that Harrison, who would have been I believe single and the youngest brother, must have had a friendship with the young school teacher. I did remember that my grandpa told me that Cone had once been a small town south of Milan during the 1860s. I hoped I would find out more about Harrison and Katie Welch.

Although I had no idea how long I had been in the attic, I was not ready to stop reading.

I picked up the next letter, which appeared to be quite long.

Near Middleton
Maryland
Monday, September 15, 1862

Our Dear Parents,

I'm taking my pen in hand to write after our regiment saw its first battle yesterday. They say that we had our baptism of fire and all we can say is Amen! I'll try and retrace our steps from last week to today.

Last Monday the regiment had orders to march from Washington City and headed into Maryland. There had been talk of the Confederates moving north. We reached Leesburg and were issued tents. Schuyler, Harrison, James Masters and me shared a tent. Our Regiment became part of the Ninth Corps led by General Reno under Generals Burnside and McClellan. We didn't stay long at Leesburg.

On the 10th we continued marching and got to a place called Brookville. The 17th become part of the 1st Brigade of Colonel Christ and General Willcox's 1st Division, 9th Corps. We also have the 8th Michigan, 28th Mass, 50th Penn and 79th New York Regiment in our brigade. By Saturday we had marched to Middletown. On the march we saw a whole lot of campfires. It was looking like a field of lightning bugs, but was really the rest of McClellan's army. Passing through Middletown the townspeople gave out some cakes, bread and water. But we came through too late and most of the food was gone. We heard artillery fire ahead.

We marched along the turnpike and I saw some really pretty countryside. The corn was ready for picking and every field had a fence or stone wall around it. To get across South Mountain our brigade was marching on what was called Old Sharpsburg Road to Fox's Gap.

And early in the morning we saw the enemy and had a fight on our hands. About noontime our regiment was posted on the right of a road. Our job was to protect some of our artillery. Rebel attacks then commenced something terrible. Sometime after 4 o'clock Colonel Withington, our regimental commander, ordered us to charge the rebels who were behind a stone wall. We then charged and with heavy yelling and firing on our part we pushed the rebs back and captured some of them.

By the beginning of dusk the fight was about over. Captain Campbell and a squad of men from Company E set out at sunset to search the woods for wounded or killed federals. I have to say we lost some good men. Myron Hawley and Dan Hopkins were wounded. Alex McKinnon, Robert Irvin and Will Woodward killed. And General Reno was killed by sharpshooter fire after the battle was over. We know that we stood proud yesterday and proved ourselves in our first fight. But folks I also saw some sights of battle I wished I hadn't seen. Schuyler and Harrison and me came out of this alright, but we saw the elephant and aint anxious to see what today brings. I must now end for I hear the bugle's call to form up for today's march.

I Hear the Bugle's Call

Near Antietam Creek
Friday, September 19, 1862

By the time you get this letter your probably have heard of a great battle the Ninth Corps has been in here in Maryland. That battle has been why I didn't finish and get this letter done sooner. I'll start out first with some bad news. On Wednesday during the fighting Schuyler got wounded. From what I see he's doing fine. He was shot in his left leg. He was hit pretty hard, but he told us he doesn't think he will lose his leg, Thank God. He is in a field hospital not far from here. Harrison and I went to see him this morning. He is feeling some pain, but the doctors say that there's a good chance he will be walking again. Ma, try to get over and see Lomira, she doesn't know about Schuyler yet. He's gonna write her soon as he's able. He says to tell her don't worry none he's alright. And Ma, Schuyler says not to worry none. He'll be fine in a while. Here's how it happened. On Wednesday our regiment was moved west near a place called Sharpsburg, Maryland. That morning a huge battle broke out near a place called Antietam Creek. Though the battle started in the morning our corps was held out till later in the afternoon. About one o'clock our regiment was ordered across a bridge over the creek. We had some hard fighting ahead of us. We crossed the bridge then marched toward the town. This is when Schuyler got hit. He went down with a few others, but we got help for him and saw that he was taken back to the surgeon's tent. We fought with the other regiments almost to the town of Sharpsburg. But heavy Confederate artillery fire kept us pinned down. We spent the night in the field. Folks, I do say it was might painful to hear the groans of the wounded and see the mangled bodies of our men and the rebels laying around us. And the sights I saw was something awful. Shot and shells pierced the trees and the fences were riddled by bullets. I dare say the earth looked like it was plowed by the artillery shells that hit. Bodies of both Union and rebel soldiers littered the field. I saw a dead rebel officer with sword in hand as if to lead one more charge. And the most pitiful sight was of a dead Union soldier no more than a boy holding his canteen for one final drink. And it got to be a might cold without our tent and no cooking fires for the night. Thursday the rebels retreated back across the Potomac and we marched back across the Antietam where we are now. We were told we was the victors in this but I don't know. We heard the 17th had around eighteen killed and with Schuyler near about ninety wounded. We all hope that this battle will be our last for the season.

I've Seen the Elephant!

If not forever. The loss of life we're seeing can't go on. There's already talk of preparing for winter quarters. But we pray the war will end soon. Our spirits are still high and our cause is righteous but we seen too much death and misery in just a couple of weeks. Harrison and I both hope everyone is well back home. We hope to see our mail soon. We hadn't seen any for weeks. We'll write again soon.

> Your loving sons,
>
> Daniel and Harrison
> 17th Mich Vol Regiment
> 9th Corps
> Army of the Potomac

After reading this letter I know I had just found a key piece to my family's history. These three brothers had just been one of the bloodiest battles of the Civil War. This must have been how Schuyler became wounded and perhaps this explains the cane I found in the trunk.

Each letter I read became a page of clues for a mystery that I suspect will surprise me and my family.

I then began reading a letter dated Monday, October 6, 1862. My Dear Lomira and children…

> Camp A General Hospital
> Frederick Maryland
> Monday October 6, 1862

My Dear Lomira and Children,

As you may have heard I have been wounded. Now don't fret none cause I'm resting just fine. Though you will see my handwriting is different. My strength is a little on the weak side so I have help with this letter writing from Mr. Cheever who is with the Christian Commission. They are a group of church people helping here at the hospital. I'll try to explain what happened. On the 14th of September our regiment saw the rebels for the first time at a placed called Fox's Gap at South Mountain, Maryland. We saw some heavy action, but we drove the rebs back. You would have been proud of the McFall Brothers. We put the fear in them rebs. We lost some good men at this fight. We saw battle for the first time and I ain't afraid to say I was more than a little nervous, but we felt the Lord's spirit on our side. Then we kept marching south and as you may have heard we was involved in a large battle near Antietam Creek.

The battle began early in the morning, but our regiment didn't get into it until the afternoon. Early in the forenoon we crossed over Antietam Creek on a bridge that was fought over all morning. We then were ordered to spread out and push the rebs back to town. As me and Daniel and Harrison moved out we got noticed by the rebs and shots came around us like bees around the hive. I then felt my left leg get knocked like a mule kick. The blow knocked me to the ground. That's when I saw I'd been hit.

Daniel and Harrison came to me, but I told them I was all right. They said they would check on me as soon as they could. Sometime after that I must have passed out cause the next thing I know I was lying in a barn and some army surgeon was looking at my leg. Lomira dear, do not worry about me. The Lord is with me. I see and hear the sounds of men a heap worse off than me.

Daniel and Harrison came through the battle unhurt and they saw me before I was taken by wagon to Frederick City and this hospital. I must confess that wagon ride back to the hospital was one ride I hope never to repeat.

I've been getting good care here, but I don't know how long I'll be staying here. The doctors tell me my wound will heal. Nobody knows how long that'll take. I don't think you need worry the young ones about me. You can write me here at the hospital for I suspect I'll be here awhile. Pass these words on to John and my parents. Tell em don't worry none. We are all in God's hands dear wife. Kiss the children for me.

Your loving husband,
Schuyler

My initial reaction after reading this letter was one of elation. As with the other letters this letter contained some people and terms I knew nothing about. But like pieces of a puzzle, this included some clues to my family's story that I did begin to

I've Seen the Elephant!

understand. If I had this right, here was Schuyler McFall's letter to his wife telling her of his battle wound and the other letters told of the brothers as they faced battle for the first time.

This packet of letters began to tell me what was occurring in the life of the McFall's. In addition I was learning what these men and their families were like as real people--not just names on grave stones.

Knowing that, I had to read on. I picked up the rest of the packet and continued with a letter dated October 15, 1862 from Paint Creek

Paint Creek, Michigan
Wednesday October 15, 1862

My Dearest Husband,

How sad and shocked I was to read your letter of 6th inst. I pray you are in good health and are healing. Since reading of your wounding, I have tried to keep good thoughts as I know He is looking out for your well being. As soon as I could, I drove over to your parents and shared the news. They said that they had heard from Daniel and Harrison and were about to come and tell me. I tried to show them that I was certain of your recovery, but Schuyler, I do worry. Your parents wanted me to tell you that they are praying for your recovery and hope as I do the Army will send you home to recover with us. I do my best to keep your condition from Elenora and Preston. When they ask about you I smile and say Papa's coming home soon. Oh I wish that was true! I also shared the news with John and Emma. They too send their prayers and hope for your quick recovery.

I have another reason for wanting you home soon. I believe we will be adding to our family, Dear Husband. I believe I am with child once more. Although it is early I believe the signs will prove true. So we can see that God wants us together soon, safe and healthy. I have yet to tell this wonderful news to anyone.

Thomas and John have been bringing in the corn crop and the orchard has been very abundant this year. Thomas believes we can make a good profit from the cider and he and John have been selling a good deal of cord wood.

I Hear the Bugle's Call

Samantha has been a great help with the housekeeping and I expect to need her more in the months ahead. I trust you will find enclosed with this letter some stamps, envelopes and other surprises.

We here at home are very proud of what you and the boys are doing for our country. And we pray this tragic war ends soon. Please do as the doctors say and write me as often as you can.

With love from your children and myself,
Lomira

Paint Creek, Michigan
Thursday, October 16, 1862

Dear Brothers,

It is with deep concern and sadness I write these words to you boys. Lomira has told Emma and me about Schuyler's wounding in battle. She tells us he describes his condition as not to bad, but he may not be telling us all he knows. We know you and Harrison will be looking in on him as much as you can. Ma and Pa are worried of course and we all look forward to hearing from you boys about Schuyler's well being. Write us as soon as you can and let us know how he is doing and if we can send him anything to help his suffering.

Daniel, I've been working your farm and mine as we've had a busy harvest. Though its been dry lately we had a good corn crop on your east ten acres and my south ten. We hear that there is a government agent in Ypsilanti buying grain for the Army. Thomas, and I are going to take the corn to the Paint Creek Mill then up to Ypsilanti. Pass this next part on to Schuyler. Schuyler, you'd be real proud of Lomira and how she's looking after the farm and the young ones too. I know she misses you and prays for your recovery and return home as soon as you can.

Me and Emma are doing fine though I've had a time doctoring a couple of ailing calves. Emma sends her best to all of you and we are proud of your brave duty to our state and country.

Brother John

I've Seen the Elephant!

Camp A, General Hospital
Frederick, Maryland
Saturday, October 25, 1862

My dear Lomira and Children,

I received your letter of the 15th inst. which I read with great joy. The news you tell of a possible family member is the best medicine I could have. I pray that God continues to be kind to us.

I am still in Frederick and getting better. As you can tell I do not have enough strength in my hands to hold a pen, so Mr. Cheever continues to show his kindness and write the words I tell him. My leg wound is healing, but my strength is still not completely strong. The hospital is a large one with many patients, most from the Antietam battle. I have seen a few from Company E and its good to be around friends in a place like this. I've seen Ed Haight, Henry Burr and Robert Wheeler. They all seem to be on the mend. Daniel and Harrison I hear are on the march back to Virginia. If the rumors hold true, maybe this infernal war will end soon.

The nights here are the most troublesome to me. I lie here thinking of you and our dear young ones and how we would spend the nights with you reading to them and I rocking with my pipe. I trust we can relive those times again soon. Please keep me up on the farm news and what's going on in the area.

There is a woodcarver that comes into the hospital. For two dollars he carves a cane that looks first rate. He can put whatever a person wants. I think the next time he comes by I'll see what he can make for me. It might be my only war souvenir of this war if you don't count a gimpy leg. Mr. Cheever tells me it's about time for lights out so I must end this.

Write soon and hug the children for me.

Your loving husband,
Schuyler

I Hear the Bugle's Call

Near Berlin, Virginia
Monday, October 27, 1862

Our dear Parents,

Well, much has been happening here since I last wrote. We'd been marching a whole lot and when I think I have time to write we get the call to form up and begin to marching again. Tell John we got his letter of 16th inst. and we were pleased with the news of home. It's at night when we have a time to rest and we hear fiddle playing or singing we think of home and kinfolk. A couple of weeks ago we marched near Frederick City and me and Harrison got a chance to look up Schuyler. He's looking better and seems to be improving. He says his leg is mending but he may be limping awhile. We kidded him that if he showed more of a waddle he could be going home. He said the doctors aren't sure yet how much of a recovery he'll have. We couldn't stay long but we gave him some writing stuff and a few other things we picked up at the sutler's post.

Since I last wrote, I'm sure you've heard more of the battle at Antietam Creek. Beside Schuyler's wounding a few others of our boys got messed up like Henry Burr, Ed Haight and Robert Vining. We hear they will survive their wounds, but not for poor Gilbert Peck and Webster Ruckman, good brave boys they were. By the way, James Masters has become our tent mate with Schuyler's absence. He sends his regards. If you want to know what our daily camp routine is like—here it is. At daylight is drum beat for our first roll call. At 8 o'clock we start up a breakfast of usually coffee, bacon and biscuits from 8 a.m. until 10 a.m. Company drill. From 10 till 3 p.m. time for ourselves which is taken up with cleaning our equipment, noon meal and mending our uniform. From 3 p.m. till 5 p.m. Brigade drill then a dress parade, supper and tattoo at 9 p.m. In fact, a few weeks ago we were reviewed by President Lincoln, Generals McClellan and Burnside. The President is a homely man, but his face is that of an honest soul.

Last week Colonel Withington's wife sent the regiment some pepper. We all got a part of it. It sure makes the food taste better. On the last Sabbath some of the company had been called on to sing by the chaplain. It does bring back thoughts of Sundays at home.

Our company clerk, Austin George, will be going home soon. He's the man

I've Seen the Elephant!

with only one arm that helped start Company E. He couldn't stay any longer. We Augusta boys have asked him to look in on our families if he could. Hope he'll look you folks up and meets the family.

We hear rumors of possible change at the top. General McClellan may get replaced by our own General Burnside. General Willcox might take over for Burnside. We just hope someone will lead us to that last battle—the one that ends this infernal war. The number one question here is where's our pay? No one volunteered to fight for free!

Harrison is doing well. Folks, I think you'd be pretty proud of the boy, he has grown up a lot. We both have seen some awful sights and had to put up with a lot especially now winter is coming but we also know the enemy we face and what could happen if we lower our flag—that won't happen!

We'll write again when we can.

> Your sons, Harrison and Daniel
> Company E
> 17th Michigan Vol. Regiment

> Paint Creek, Michigan
> Wednesday, October 29, 1862

Dear Daniel and Harrison,

I want to take this opportunity to express my prayers and those of our church for your continued good health and safety. Lomira has told me of Schuyler's wounding and our prayers go daily for his rapid recovery. I will be writing to him soon to express our good wishes.

I have read about the 17th Michigan Regiment and congratulate you boys for your heroic efforts for our State and Country. We are proud of all of our boys from Augusta and look forward to seeing you march home soon. I've been told that Company E has in its ranks good Christian men and with you three I have no doubt. The Ladies Society is preparing a gift of socks, blankets and other incidentals for your company. They should arrive soon before the winter season arrives. We here back home hear of peace rumors and we continue to pray that they come true. We pray that the Confederates will learn that our

I Hear the Bugle's Call

Union will be preserved and with the President's recent proclamation will enjoy new freedom for all. Please write when you have the opportunity. I will share such communication with the Congregation.

> In God's Name,
>
> Pastor Neal Hoover
> First Congregational Church
> And Society of Augusta

> Paint Creek
> Wednesday, November 5, 1862

My Dearest Husband,

I was so grateful and relieved to receive yours letter of the 25th ult. All of us here have been praying daily for your rapid recovery and your improving condition is welcome news. I hope you have been doing everything the doctors tell you to do. We hear reports that the conditions in army hospitals are not always what they should be. We pray your hospital may be one of the better ones. Thank Mr. Cheever for being your right-hand man while you get stronger.

And I do have wonderful news for you. It is true that we will be adding to our family in the new year! It is certain that I am with child and the family has taken the news with great joy. So we have a very important reason for your full recovery and a return home. Do not worry over me. Thomas and Samantha have lessened my burdens a great deal. When possible I continue to read to Elenora and Preston. I continue to answer their questions about papa with "he'll be home soon."

John and Thomas tell me that the corn brought in a good price this fall as did the orchard crops. And they have laid away a good supply of wood for the winter.

Samantha and me have been busy preserving and our cellar looks pretty full.

I've been to your parents a few days ago and they are doing well. They are thinking of you of course and worry a great deal. John has been doing a good job taking care of them. John has written to Daniel and Harrison recently and hopes to hear from them soon. We read in the paper the Army of the Potomac is marching back to Virginia. We sure pray this scourge of a war ends soon.

I do hope you can get a cane made for you. I bet we would look right smart walking into church with that cane if only for appearance not for need. I'm sending you some new socks and a blanket that were made by some of the church ladies.

I will close now as I get ready to turn in. As always I'll give the little ones "papa's kiss."

Love from your children and Lomira

As I finished the last letter in the packet, I tried to make some sense in what I've read and what I had experienced. I again picked up Daniel and Harrison's letter written to their parents. As I began to reread the telling of their first taste of battle I heard,…"Okay little brothers let's get this gear packed up quick like." Hearing this I look up and again I saw Schuyler and he's talking to Harrison. It appears I had somehow mysteriously become Daniel McFall once again.

But this time this strange fantasy is different. The last packet of letters I read described battles and death. Would I as Daniel McFall be witness to the real scenes of war? Would I observe my brother being seriously wounded and others that I know also wounded or horribly killed? I don't believe I have the ability to change what will happen nor warn them what is to take place. Why would they believe such a tale? As Daniel I may well be transported through these events and trust in his skill, character, luck, and God's will.

I hastily packed our gear to be ready to move out. Sergeant Maltman appeared at our tent and said to be ready for company formation, leave the tent it'll catch up with us later. It's early September and it appears our training is over, it's time to meet the rebels.

I fell into formation with Harrison and Schuyler—our knapsacks weighing us down like we are carrying cordwood. We still have our foreign muskets though rumor says that'll change soon.

As we started out of Washington, we marched northwest to Maryland not

I Hear the Bugle's Call

south to Virginia. As I looked around, I said to Schuyler, "When we are marching like this I see the other companies with us the scene strikes me hard," "We Michigan boys and the others make up a powerful looking force." "Maybe so, said Schuyler, "but where we're going there's bound to be some fellas who aint so impressed."

Not far out of town we heard some of the Normal boys begin singing, "John Browns Body." Harrison started to join in though he didn't know all the words at first. Schuyler and I looked at each other and said "what the hell" and we join in. It wasn't exactly the church choir back home but it did pass the time down the dusty roads of Maryland.

We marched through the night stopping only for short breaks. Early the next morning we reached Leesburg. Finally we had time to start cooking fires for coffee, bacon and biscuits. During the day our tents arrived. Sergeant Maltman came by to assign a few from Company E to picket duty. Luckily the McFall clan wasn't chosen.

Early the next morning we broke camp and the march continued. We privates aren't told much, but we did hear that Lee and his force was marching North and we were in pursuit.

During the day's march we caught up with some other regiments including the 8th Michigan. During the day we had a break so Harrison, Schuyler and I visited some of the Michigan boys in the 8th. They told us they enlisted a year before us and had seen too many battles led by too many incompetent officers. As we walked back to our tent, I told Harrison and Schuyler, "We can only hope we won't be saying that same thing."

Reveille was well before sunrise. We marched all day reaching a place called Damascus at sunset. As we begin to start our cooking fires James Masters says to us, "Sure wish we would be getting some mail soon," Harrison added, "now we know what division we'll be part of maybe that'll speed up us getting word from home." We were told that we'd be marching early next morning so we ate our rations, seen to our muskets and equipment, and turned in early. We were lucky we weren't called out for picket duty this night.

Early Friday morning (I believe it was the 12th of September) we again formed up and marched through the day. We've been marching a few days now and it's surprising to see how much dirt is kicked up by horses, mules, and humans along a march. By the end of day it's hard to identify anyone through the cover of dust and mud on uniforms, faces and equipment.

We camped at New Market near a creek. We finally had time to refill our canteens, and wash up some. We spent the night there and Harrison and James Masters were called out for picket duty. They went out about 10 to 30 rods from our camp to watch for any reb visitors. They came in after midnight as they were relieved by others from the company.

The next day, Saturday, we formed up again and began marching. I mentioned to Schuyler, "I hear thunder in the west, but I see no storm," "I do too, and Daniel and I'm thinkin what we're hearing is a man made storm not of my liking," he replied back.

By mid-afternoon we stopped our march at Middletown. As we looked out ahead into a valley, what I scene I beheld! Thousands of campfires and tents covered the valley floor. James Masters remarked, "My God it looks like a city of canvas down there." "This sure is a sight I aint soon to forget," added Harrison. As we marched through Middletown we heard the townspeople handed out some cakes and water earlier, but as we were coming in late we missed out on most of the benefits. As we were marching through town, Schuyler looked over to me and said, "Hey look at the church, what I wouldn't give to be back listening to Pastor Hoover back home right now." All I could say was, "Amen brother" to that idea.

We could hear artillery fire ahead of us as we marched west out of town.

Early reveille on this Sunday. We had a quick breakfast of roasted corn, crackers and coffee. Not my favorite choice of a meal but I was getting use to the army diet.

The roads were crowded with horses, wagons, artillery and soldiers. We were following what was called the National Road towards Sharpsburg. Off in the distance was South Mountain. A place that we would find very dangerous before the day was through. This was pretty farm country, Schuyler remarked "look how good the corn is, and I've never seen so much land fenced in my by stone walls." I replied, "I would sure like to see that hay sitting in my loft back home."

As the morning went on the sun was rising higher in the sky and so was the temperature. We turned on a road and there high on a ridge we saw signal flags and riders scurrying to who knows where. Sergeant Maltman said to us,

"I'd say look sharp boys, we've got McClellan, Burnside and who knows who else watching us march along kicking up dust. Let's show'em how Michigan men can march."

Once we passed the ridge, we started to see wounded men coming our way. Some were limping or led by a friend. The cries and sounds coming from these walking wounded was something we hadn't heard before.

It was getting close to noon and Colonel Withington halted us and placed us behind some artillery along a road. No sooner had we deployed when the artillery near us started firing. We'd never been so close to such a scene before and I yelled to both Schuyler and Harrison, "We aint heard nothing like this back home!" And the smoke from those big guns started to burn our eyes something awful! To our left was a regiment from New York who after seeing us in our still new uniforms call out "fresh fish," reminding us of our not so veteran appearance. At about this time Schuyler says, "Take a good look out front boys, with that we get a glimpse for the first time of men in dirty brown and gray. The Rebs were coming at the artillery battery near us.

The 17th was then ordered to cross the road and advance to a cornfield while we hear musket rounds coming from the woods ahead. We were ordered to lay down in the cornfield while artillery battle commenced.

After a short while Colonel Withington led the regiment back along a road to the rear of the cornfield. While we were marching the action was too swift for words. I and my brothers looked at each other when we could, our facial expressions said it all, this is war, no more parades and speeches.

We are ordered to attack Confederates behind a stone wall at the edge of a pasture. While we charged the wall the rebs retreated. We gain the wall and look ahead. Ahead were rebs lined up firing. Colonel Withington ordered "Forward men" then "fix bayonets" was heard. My heart was pounding and my throat was as dry as dust. I looked to my right was Harrison and to my left was Schuyler. We all had the same appearance of alarm but also determination.

We soon climbed over a wall once defended by the enemy, there was our foe. It now became a man to man fight with shell, bayonet, rifle butt and fists. I came upon one reb who had just fired his musket over my head and with a sharp lunge my bayonet caught him under his left shoulder and down he went. I then quickly spotted Schuyler and Harrison along with James Masters showing they could handle a bayonet as well.

What seemed like minutes actually lasted about an hour or so. The rebs retreated and the battle ended. Some of the regiment pursued the retreating men taking some prisoners. But Company E was ordered to stay put, look after our casualties and equipment.

By the end of the battle it was near late afternoon. Later we were ordered to the supply wagons in the rear as our cartridge pouches were near empty.

We moved back down from the gap that night. No fires were lit for fear of sharpshooters so we ate our biscuits and beans cold. As night was coming on, I sat with Harrison, Schuyler, James Masters and a few other Michigan men. We shared our thoughts on the day.

We looked at each other in the faint sunlight and none of us looked like we did when the day started.

Schuyler was the first to speak, "We've been through one hell of a fight today." Jim Masters replied, "you've said it all my friend." Each one of us was covered in dust, sweat and gun powder. Although we were plenty tired we were also aware of what we accomplished. We faced the enemy for the first time and drove them off the field. I guess that means we're the victor and we showed them us new guys could stand and fight. We know we probably lost some good men today but we ended the day feeling proud of our regiment and our company.

Before the battle, we were told by some who came before us the one day "we'd see the elephant." As we sat in the day's twilight we all agreed today was that day.

The next morning word spread that General Reno had been killed yesterday by a sharpshooter. Hearing the news, I said to my brothers, "Well it makes no difference whether you're a general or a private, if there's a minie ball with your name on it, it'll find you." Upon hearing me Harrison opened up his cartridge pouch and holds a minie-ball in his hand. And with a slight smile replied, "Now look at how small this is, aint no name such as Harrison McFall gonna fit on one of those."

I knew that word of this battle might find the newspapers and the family back home might be worried. Speaking for Harrison and myself, I wrote home to our parents telling them what had happened. When I wrote home I told them of the facts but tried to leave out as much of the images of battle as I could. Ma and Pa don't need to know what ghastly scenes erupt on a battlefield.

We heard the bugle's call which ended Harrison's attempt at humor. Our company began to form up which we guessed meant we're moving out. We've been through the fire of battle for the first time and held up pretty fair. Am I and my brothers ready for what comes next?

As we move out I become almost sick to my stomach as we march through some of yesterday's battlefield. As I glance back at my brothers I can see they look as shocked as me. Both armies spent the Sabbath trying to kill each other. This must be God's will as punishment to both armies.

As we marched west and then south, we spotted dead artillery horses and damaged caissons on our left and right. And mixed in those scenes are the bodies of dead soldiers mostly—rebels yet to be buried. Above all of the horrible sights was the odor of death and dying through which had to march. And the sight of vultures leading their attack on the battlefield. James Masters marching to my side said in a low voice, "Let's get movin outta here," Schuyler overhears and replied "Amen to that thought. I don't think I'll be forgetting this stench for some time."

By Tuesday the 16th of September our brigade had marched to a small village called Portertown. We stopped and some of the regiment went out on picket duty. As we made our afternoon meal, we could hear the occasional musket fire in the distance. Although it sounded some distance away we were always alert for that stray bullet coming from somewhere. Wednesday's reveille sounded early and we marched without time for breakfast or coffee. Our brigade was to be held in reserve for a battle we knew was coming. We were near a place called Antietam Creek.

We could see a lot of men and artillery moving ahead and the thunder of cannon is near. This certainly looked like the big battle we thought was coming had arrived. Captain Campbell told our men that the regiment was to be held in reserve with the whole brigade as the fighting began. I and my brothers were nervously sitting on the ground checking and rechecking our musket and cartridge boxes. And we made sure our canteens were full. No one knows when we'll get a sight of clean water today, Harrison looked over at Schuyler and me and said, "ya know, we aint been soldiers for very long but we've done ourselves proud," but if something happens to me tell Pa and

I've Seen the Elephant!

Ma." "Hold up now," replied Schuyler, "as you said we've learned our job as soldiers damn well, and us McFalls can take care of ourselves. We're gonna come through this day first rate so no need for speeches." With that Schuyler glanced at me with a look that I read as determined. I uttered an "amen" and stated, "If Harrison McFall can't fit on a bullet neither can Daniel or Schuyler." Both smiled my way and nodded in agreement.

Close to noon our regiment moved up slowly to an area closer to Antietam Creek. Since morning there had been a large battle taking place north of our position. We heard the thunder of artillery for hours.

At about 2 p.m. our brigade received orders to cross the stone bridge up ahead and form up on the right flank after we crossed.

Our company crossed the bridge and we could see the fight that took place earlier. As we doubled quick across the bridge we were stepping around and over wounded Union men and I must also say more than a few brave men whose last breath of life was taken on this bridge.

We crossed quickly and our brigade fanned out to the right near a farmhouse. As we were moving forward we were quickly hit with artillery fire coming from high ground west of the road. At this point the action around our company really started heating up. As I and my brothers started to crouch down behind some fence rails, I saw Schuyler stand then swivel to his left, then fall giving off short yelp. I shouted to Harrison and James Masters. "Schuyler's hit!" I being the closest was able to get to him and see he was alive but in pain. His left leg was bloodied, but still intact. I wrapped a bandana above the knee as a tourniquet and gave him my canteen. I told him lay still and we'd see after him as soon as we can.

Our company continued to attack, but the rebel fire was slowing us down. By then end of the afternoon, the attack was called off and we moved back to near the Antietam bridge where the attack started. As nightfall came, we had to camp right where we sat. No fires, no hot food. Harrison and I asked Captain Campbell if we could go and find what happened to Schuyler but he said we couldn't move but he'd do his best to check with the field hospital. The night was cold out there with no fires and for most no blankets. But the worst of the night wasn't the cold but the moans—the pleadings for water or the calling for loved ones by the wounded of both sides was the worst. There is no glory in witnessing such a scene.

I Hear the Bugle's Call

On the 19th of September we marched toward the Potomac River as General Lee's army had retreated south back to Virginia. With the battle over camp life became more routine. We camped near Antietam Furnace. Now we were able to wash for the first time in a few days and hot coffee and biscuits tasted pretty good. About this time Captain Campbell called us together to talk about what we'd just experienced. The Captain formed us up by his tent and began by saying "men we've been through two devilish battles together. The rebels we faced were veterans and well led. But Company E and the Seventeenth Michigan stood up to them with bravery and spirit. We've lost some good friends and neighbors. We won't forget them and their courage. Generals McClellan, Willcox and Colonels Christ and Withington all expressed to me their commendation for the valor shown by this regiment. "The rebels have gone south which allows a time for us to rest and refit. We may be heading to Virginia."

Harrison and I did get a chance to see Schuyler at the field hospital before he was taken east. We thought he was asleep when we came by him, but he was awake and told us not to worry none. He said his leg will be just fine and he'll be back with us in a short time. Harrison and I had a chance to talk to a doctor who stated, "Your brother has been seriously wounded, but with care I don't think he'll lose the leg." "He'll be laid up for awhile and I can't guarantee for how long." Before we left we told Schuyler we'd write home to tell our parents what happened and they shouldn't worry none.

Before our regiment marched back East, we had a grand review by President Lincoln and all the generals. What a show we put on! We got issued some clean uniforms and we shined our rifles and brass and we looked ready for a 4th of July parade back home. We marched past the President and I was able to glance at the man as we marched by. His clothes looked a bit lived in and his long arms outstretched his coat sleeves some. What I could see of his face I saw a worn down look and his eyes had the look of concern.

By late October we had marched into Virginia and hoped to prepare for winter quarters. Harrison and I did get to see Schuyler as he was sent to a larger army hospital at Frederick, Maryland. We saw how he had been improving, but still was weak and not able to move about much.

While I have been with the company, I and Harrison and Schuyler had struck up a friendship with a man from Ypsilanti named Austin George. He's quite the interesting character. He had lost an arm as a young boy but his infirmity never slowed him down. He was our company's first clerk and helped organize it from the start. Because of this loss he wasn't allowed to officially join, but he has been with us from the start and doing a first rate job. Unfortunately, he can't stay any longer and returned home. My brothers and I really enjoyed his company and we asked him to look in on our families when he could.

As October neared the end we heard of a shake-up at the top. It seems General McClellan may be replaced by our own commander, General Burnside. Harrison and James Masters agree with me that as simple privates we know little of strategy and all the politics. We can only hope that the people who do, make the right decisions. We shall see.

As the month of October ends I found myself and Company E in Berlin, Virginia. We had begun to prepare for winter. Harrison, me, James Masters and the Hardy brothers found enough tent canvas and wood rails for a tolerable hut for winter. We'd been called only a few times when rebel cavalry were spotted but it came to nothing. Being closer to Washington City improved our food rations and hot coffee goes well on these now cold fall mornings.

On Tuesday after afternoon drill, Sergeant Maltman told me and Harrison we've been assigned picket duty for the night. So before sundown we moved out of the camp about five or six hundred yards to relieve the pickets on duty. The password for the night was "Wolverine" with the accepted countersign "Huron."

The evening came early and a clear sky produced an almost full moon. Harrison and I took turns staying awake but for awhile we both scanned through the twilight. Our picket site had a good earth berm with branches for cover. As I peered ahead I began to spot movement. I quickly alerted Harrison in barely a whisper, "Brother, look quick to the tree line!" Harrison responded "Something or things moving our way but I can't make out what." My senses are now on full alert with a heart pounding to match. I brought my rifle closer to my side. As the objects came closer Harrison and I were about to issue our warning shots.

I Hear the Bugle's Call

A Soldier's Winter
November 1862—March 1863

The movement in the tree line grew more threatening with no countersign heard to calm the nerves of the Yankee privates. We heard the breaking of twigs on the ground by what sounded like heavy boots not more than fifty yards ahead of our position.

We didn't know if we're facing a lone soldier or a squad of Johnnies. What we did know was they weren't responding to our charges and they're headed our way.

I told Harrison, "If what comes out of those shadows aint friendly, we fire!"

As a sign of good luck, the moon had evaded the cover of the clouds as the enemy emerged from the woodline.

Harrison and I had our rifles at the ready when out steps a Guernsey cow followed obediently behind by two calves. As I looked over to Harrison as he lowered his rifle, I said with a grin, "Brother, I don't bet we'll be writing home about his battle." He replied back, "maybe not, but if we can convince these 'Sesech' to surrender, then I know of some men back in camp who might declare our action well fought."

With that said, we allowed our "captives" to invade our picket without another challenge. They immediately surrendered to superior forces.

When our picket duty ended at sun-up we escorted our "prisoners" back to camp. And Harrison was right. The response from our company when they saw our captives was as spirited as if we were marching in General Lee himself.

I found that fall had arrived in with a hint of winter not far off. The October mornings came in with a crisp feel and what trees had escaped the soldier's ax for firewood or cabin walls, displayed leaves the varied colors of autumn.

We had been lucky to have with us a Methodist preacher by the name of Josiah Childs. Pastor Childs was from Alexandria, Virginia, but was a true union man. He had been with the 17th Michigan for about two weeks preaching on the Sabbath and helping where needed. He also had taken a trip up to Frederick, Maryland and looked in on the men from our regiment. When he returned he stopped by Harrison and me and gave us an encouraging report on Schuyler's condition. Schuyler passed on news from Lomira that he will soon be a papa again. We all agreed that news like that would surely add to his spirits and would be the best medicine he could have.

I found that following the battle at Antietam Creek the month of October was a busy one for our regiment. By month's end we had traveled from Sharpsburg to Monocacy Junction, where we guarded the B & O railroad line, then back to Virginia stopping at Warrenton. We could only guess where we were headed next.

As rebel threats on our supply lines lessened as we moved east. It also made an improvement in our meals. We were supplied pork, beans, fish and salted beef, rice, sugar, molasses, coffee, and bread. And as an added bonus, Colonel Withington's wife again sent our regiment some pepper. That pepper added some spark to our victuals which helped the cooler days of fall go by a bit easier.

A favorable turn of events had taken place. We were issued some new clothes. Each of us was issued a new shirt, a pair of pants, socks, and a pair of drawers. Also, a winter great coat came our way. Our old clothes were in pitiful shape and the constant attack by the "body guards," also called lice, was an on-going skirmish. We can only hope these invaders decide to march south and attack the rebels for awhile.

I had found that camplife had its moments of entertainment. Our company had its fair share of good voices for singing, mostly favorite hymns and folk songs. Harrison and I found some really spirited checker players. Also, card playing became a popular activity but we chose not to give in to such a fool's game.

Throughout October and November Captain Campbell had us challenge some of the other companies in our regiment to spirited competitions in wrestling, boxing and even a snowball fight. In the snowball fight James Masters, Harrison and I did our best to uphold Company E's reputation for courage and determination. We took on Company D and after the skirmish had ended we declared ourselves the winners based on the number of projectiles thrown and the disheveled look of our foe.

A Soldier's Winter, November 1862–March 1863

As the cold weather came upon us I noticed more men reporting to sick call with coughs, colds and fevers. Harrison and I agreed that the busier we are the healthier we stay. We heard that the cures the doctors prescribed could be worse than the ailments.

I had noticed that the inaction of winter camp has resulted in too many men falling for the evil of the "Devil's Drug." Alcohol does not seem to be too difficult to obtain from the sutler's wagon or selfmade by some. This homemade elixir is made from any plant or other living substance one can imagine. If this brew doesn't kill the soldier, the result usually is one powerful headache the next day. With the war on hold there appears to be too much time for some to fall for such nonsense as well as an overabundance of profanity. As I observe our regiment, although we are far from being saints, we are keeping our moral senses as best we can.

Harrison and I kept our camp routine of picket duty usually once a week. It did give us the unusual experience occasionally to talk with the rebels across from our post. It usually started out with some innocent calls such as, "Hey, rebs, aint you boys gone home yet?" To which one would respond back. "We are home, its you boys that are the unwelcome visitors." After a bit more bantering I or Harrison would yell over, "Hey rebs, got any trade goods?" A response, "Sure Yank, we got some fine Virginia tobaccy here, what you got?" Our usual trade item was coffee so I would respond, "We got the best coffee in America right here."

With the trade goods agreed upon, I or Harrison would venture out to meet our trade partner. Usually a short conversation would then take place concerning home states, families, and a mutual distrust of most officers and politicians. We sometimes exchanged newspapers or the latest army gossip. After a few minutes we then walked back to our respective pickets and the routine of war resumed.

Each time one of us participated in the trade we came away with not only tobacco or other items but also something more valuable.

As I found myself talking to a man, who perhaps is near my own age, needing a bath as much as me, but, wearing the uniform of the enemy, I'm seeing myself, Daniel McFall. I saw a man who is fighting for the wrong cause, a cause I cannot support or allow to be successful-disunion. But I began to see he had the same devotion and belief in his cause as I do for mine.

I Hear the Bugle's Call

The first time this happened I said to Harrison and James Masters, "Boys, there's a reb across the way that looks to be like us in age, and appearance, yet he's our enemy, he's as iron willed as we are. This could be a long war."

As November turned to December the cold north wind visited our camp on a daily basis. One of the men I spoke to in the 8th Michigan described this time of year from experience. He called it "a soldier's winter." It was time of short hours of daylight and long nights when memories of home were constant guests at our campfires.

Harrison and I knew it would do us no good to dwell on home and loved ones but, it wasn't easy spending the long December evenings without our thoughts traveling elsewhere.

As December 25th came nearer, the images of home and hearth occupied the minds of all the men. Thursday, December 25th, Christmas morning revealed itself in bright sunshine and finger-numbing cold. As Harrison and I started our meal of bacon, biscuits, and coffee before reveille, Harrison asked, "I sure wish I knew how Schuyler's doing on this holiday morn?" I responded back "It does pain me to think how long he's been laid up." "I do hope he and Lomira have been able to stay in touch. Hope his Christmas Day has some comfort."

Unknown to either I or Harrison, Schuyler and Lomira had kept up their writing to each other since his wounding at Antietam. Christmas in an army camp is a poor substitute for home, but spending the day in a hospital rated even lower.

Paint Creek
Thursday, December 25, 1862

My Dear Husband,

As I write this letter I am anxiously awaiting a letter from you, my dearest Schuyler. I try not to but I cannot help but worry over your injury and health. I pray our Lord is looking over you today on this special day. It does sadden me that we are apart on this most festive holiday but I will keep up a firm resolve.

A Soldier's Winter, November 1862–March 1863

I have not told the children of your injury for I do not think they are of age to understand. This morning when they looked in their Christmas stockings Elenora found some new clothes for her doll and Preston discovered a beautiful carved wooden horse—thanks to the carving skill of your brother John. This afternoon John and Emma took us over to your parents for a fine holiday meal. As we sat at the table we all spoke of our hopes that next year all the family will be at the table including our new family member. The babe continues to grow and with Samantha's help I am doing well.

John continues to hear from Daniel and Harrison. It appears the regiment has gone back to Virginia. We worry after hearing of the latest battle at Fredericksburg. The newspaper said that the regiment was not involved much in the battle and we pray so. Such a tragic loss of lives for a noble cause.

John and Thomas wanted me to mention to you that they harvested 450 to 500 bushels of corn this fall. They also said that they have been "waging war" on at least a small army of muskrats and coons along the creek.

This week I will be sending you a box of items that Samantha and I have been putting together. Included you will find more stamps, writing paper, envelopes, tobacco and some homemade "surprises." Last evening John and Emma and your parents, met us, and Samantha and Thomas for the Christmas Eve service at church. As we were singing the snow started to fall and the scene took me back to our early courting days. We will share those days again. I will end now but do not worry for us, just do as the doctors say and we will be as a family again.

> From your loving children and wife,
> Lomira

I Hear the Bugle's Call

Frederick, Maryland
Thursday, December 25, 1862

Dear Lomira and children,

Merry Christmas

As you can see by the writing I am now able to hold a pencil and make a letter that I hope you can read. I am certainly beholding to Mr. Cheever for writing my letters for me as well as bringing newspapers and making these long hospital days more tolerable. I was quite pleased to get your letter of the 5th ult with the news of our family adding a member. Your letter with that news was the best medicine I have got since I came to this place. My leg is mending good, but I still have a limp that the doctors say I'll keep for a while. I seen that woodcarver I spoke of in my last letter. He's gonna carve me a cane with my name it made with some first rate work.

We got some news about Company E and the 17th. It seems that Daniel and Harrison will be spending their first winter back in Virginia. We hear that Burnside has now taken over for McClellan. We keep hearing the rebs can't last much longer but I don't see much happening now that winter has hit.

I'm glad the fall harvest went good and you have enough to make it through the winter. I am very thankful for Thomas and Samantha and John for being there for you.

My day here at the hospital usually starts early when the nurse—a young Quaker woman named Rebekah Ward who came from New York, helps me with fixing a new bandage on my leg and gets me to get to the mess hall where we can go there to eat. They serve us coffee, biscuits, a little pork and every Sunday, some baked goods. After breakfast I report to the doctor who checks my wound. The rest of the day if I feel up to it I go around to other men and talk with them. On the Sabbath we have a Chaplain come by to lead the sermon. I find by getting busy it makes me feel more useful. When I see how bad up some of the men are my condition don't seem so bad. I keep asking the doctors about what's gonna happen to me but nobody tells me nothing. They keep saying my wound still needs healing.

The hospital has been decorated for Christmas with wreaths and pretty ornaments. But it all makes me sad and feel like I need to be home with you and the young ones. I will end now as a choir from the local church has come in to sing to us.

I look forward to reading your next letter soon.

Kiss the babes for me.

> Your loving husband,
> Schuyler

It being a holiday our camp duties were few except the constant task of keeping warm and dry. For the lucky soldiers not on picket duty, which fortunately included me and my tentmates, an afternoon program was conducted by some members of the Christian Commission. These citizens provided our company with a holiday feast of roast chicken, fish, sweet potatoes, bread, cakes and the best coffee we've had in months. Harrison and I agreed, if only Pa was sitting at our table with his pipe, spewing smoke rings, we'd feel at home.

A church choir from Washington came down to sing carols and as our company is known for its voices, we joined in. We may not win any singing contests but spending the day in song and forgetting the war for a while, was a day well cherished.

Later, before tattoo sounded I sat with Harrison and composed a letter to John and family.

> Thursday, December 25, 1862

Dear Parents and Brother John and Emma, and Sisters,

I again take pen and hand to write to all of our dear kinfolk on this holiday. As I write this letter Harrison is by my side adding his thoughts to my words. We pray that this letter finds all of you in fine health.

Since I wrote last in October our Company has moved from Maryland south to Virginia. As you folks have probably read there was a huge storm of a battle here a few days ago. Our old corps commander, General Burnside replaced General McClellan. The plan was to cross the Rappahannock River at Fredericksburg and push the rebels back. As the battle began we were full of spirit behind Burnside. As we went through the city we helped ourselves to provisions like potatoes, corn meal and even rebel pancakes that surrendered to us. The battle commenced but the 17th Regiment and the 9th Corps saw little action. We heard later how some of the other regiments got caught in a buzzsaw of shell and shot.

On December 15th we made a new camp at the river's edge. It looks like our Army took a real pounding and we hear the blame for it flying in all directions. General Burnside, as commander, is the main target, deserved or not. I must say at this point as the winter has set in and a terrible loss has taken place our hopes for an ending to this war are low. Our camp is near where George Washington was said to have chopped down the cherry tree. We could use General Washington about now.

Professor Welch from the Normal School came by here a few weeks ago. He brought us fruit and a collection that the Normal students took up for our company. One dollar for each of us. That was a welcome surprise. One good turn of events was we finally got issued our Springfield rifles. And Pa, with this musket we could do some first rate hunting at home.

For winter quarters Harrison, James Masters, and myself has fixed up a few boards that we "arrested" from the Sesesh and with our tent we put up a tolerable structure. And even here in Virginia it gets mighty cold as the snow falls. We had a real odd sight a few days back. Late one clear cold night we seen the Northern Lights. It was a sight to behold. We were told that aint seen here much. Some says it's an omen of the future. Harrison and me don't put much stock in such nonsense.

We hear rumors that once Spring comes the Ninth Corps may be sent along the South's coast. But we aint paying no mind to these stories yet. We aint heard about Schuyler lately so if you get news we'd appreciate sending it our way. Me and Harrison hope to get a pass and go up to Frederick City and see him before too long.

We'd sure like it if you folks could send us some dried fruits. We don't get much fruit now in winter and we are told that fruit can keep us a bit healthier.

Harrison and I draw picket duty about once every three or four days. At times we are close enough to talk with the rebel pickets. Harrison and I traded some of our coffee for some tobacco. We both feel it was an even trade. We don't talk politics with them just ask where they're from—North Carolina. And like that.

Well I got to end this as I hear the bugle's call.

>Best wishes to all,
>
>Harrison and Daniel
>Company E
>17th Michigan Vol Regiment
>9th Corps
>Falmouth, Virginia

The new year began as the old one ended, crisp, cold and with each morning came a new search for firewood. Each company sent out foraging parties scouting for new wood sources. During the second week of January, Harrison and I volunteered one day to trudge through the snow with rifle and axe hoping to locate a new woodlot. Our party of about a dozen men plotted down old farm paths with stumps poking through the snow as if it called to attention for inspection. Walking about three miles northwest from camp, we finally came across some fence rails, and a few poplars that somehow had escaped the detection by previous scouts.

Harrison and I were among the half of the party ordered to commence chopping, while the other half stood guard against any surprise rebel visitors. Having an axe in my hand instead of a rifle felt good. For a short time, I felt like I was home in my back acreage chopping wood for my own firebox. The air smelled clean and the sound of axes hitting wood was a pleasurable relief from the screams of men and animals.

We spent about two hours collecting our bounty then a march back to camp where we were happily surprised to see the mail had arrived. Second only to payday, mail call is the most waited event. We seem to send more mail than we receive. Everyone in our tent agrees that there has to be someone back in Washington whose only job is to slow down the speed of the mail trains.

I found one letter from John, and Harrison also had one which he seemed anxious to read.

I Hear the Bugle's Call

Paint Creek, Michigan
Thursday, December 25, 1862

To Daniel and Harrison,

It has been awhile since you have heard from home, and me and Emma thought a letter on Christmas Day sharing our holiday with you two would be a fine idea.

We hope that this special day has found you both safe and as comfortable as possible. We read of the terrible battle that the Army of the Potomac was involved in earlier this month and we hope you both came through the battle unharmed.

The newspapers keep reporting how the rebels are getting less and less supplied and cannot hold out much longer. We know you boys know the real facts and we'd like to hear what you see and hear.

We hear from Lomira that Schuyler is mending well and hopes to be up around walking soon. Although we suspect his wound might be ending this war for him. I know everyone here would like to see him come home.

This fall Daniel, Thomas, and I, took in around 450 bushels of corn from your acreage. We plan on milling most of it and keep the rest as ear corn. We were able to take about 40 bushels of apples to the cider press in York and we sold most of the cider within a few weeks.

We met Lomira and the young ones at church last night for Christmas Eve service. We all said a special prayer that you and all the men from the area would be with us next Christmas.

Ma and Pa are doing fine. They are always asking about you boys and you know Ma is a worrier. And though he won't say so, Pa is a worrying at times too about his boys.

The weather here has turned real winter like. As I write this we hear a wind blowing and there's a few inches of snow on the fields.

I'll end this now and look forward to reading a letter from you boys when you find time. We are all proud of what you and Harrison and Schuyler are doing for our country.

                                  Brother John

                                  Christmas Day
                                  Thursday, December 25, 1862

Dear Harrison,

I've been intending to write you as quick as I got your last letter but its been pretty busy around here. I know I couldn't let Christmas go by without writing. I pray that this day finds you safe and well. We've been reading that the Army of the Potomac had taken quite a setback at Fredericksburg and I hope you and Daniel made it through unharmed. I hear some of the Michigan Regiments like the 16th got hit pretty bad. We at home hear that if the Army could find some better Generals this war would be over soon. But I don't know much about military things and I'll defer to your opinions on those matters.

At Cone School we had a Christmas celebration last Sunday after Sabbath service. The students (all 20 of them) and their families came by the school in the evening and we had cookies, punch, cakes, and sang carols. A light snow began to fall and I do wish you could have been here. As you can see, I did get a picture of me when a photographer from Monroe came to school to photograph the students. I hope you like it (I think my hair seems a bit unkept).

Today after church my parents and I went over to my grandparents on Farr Road for Christmas dinner. My parents have heard from your brother John, that Schuyler is progressing well in the army hospital. We do pray for his recovery and I know your family would like to see him come home if he could. We have heard of some peace rumors and we hope they come true. We here are proud of the bravery of you and your brothers.

I Hear the Bugle's Call

Please write me when you can. Let me know if there is anything I can send.

>Sincerely,
>
>Katie
>Cone, Michigan

After reading the letter from John, we both agreed it was a fine letter with good news about Schuyler and the fall harvest.

I then asked Harrison about his letter. He was a bit quiet about the author or its contents. He did finally say it was Katie Welch from Cone. He wouldn't read it to me but did say it was a "nice" letter. I did notice that something else was in the envelope. He kept the envelope close in hand, but I did get a quick glimpse of what I'd guess was a photograph. I then inquired, "Harrison, might that be a photo of a young lady?" His response was a rather nonchalant, "photo? Why there's no photo here, just a letter and some stamps." Well, I could see this situation looked interesting and worth further pursuit in the future. Not having contact with Schuyler, we were unaware of his hospital routine or his correspondence home.

>Wednesday, January 14, 1863

Dear Lomira and Children,

I received your Christmas letter and package with much happiness. Although I am much stronger I still have a weakness in my hand which still requires my asking for someone with a stronger hand. Therefore a kind Christian man by the name Leonard Neumann from Frederick City is writing this letter for me. Mr. Cheever who had been helping me was called to help his kin in Baltimore. I trust this letter finds you and the young ones healthy and safe. I sure missed not being with you on Christmas. Here at the hospital there was a fine service and two church choirs sang carols. It surely made me think of being at our Christmas service back home.

A Soldier's Winter, November 1862–March 1863

If you remember I told you of a woodcarver who carves canes for the patients for a small cost. Well I had him carve me one and its first rate. Its made of walnut and has my name etched on the top along side of it is the serpent Secession. He charged me only two dollars and I plan on bringing it home to show.

I do hope you are taking care of yourself in your condition. You call on Thomas or Samantha for any help with chores.

My leg is healing fine. I am able to walk with help a little more each week.

I am getting bored and anxious to move on. If you could please send some newspapers for I have little to read here. The Bible we got in Ypsilanti has been a fine companion. The weather here in Maryland is much like Michigan, but with less snow. I see out the windows a few inches of snow, but no drifts.

The doctors still do not tell me nothing about when I can leave. I have heard from Daniel and Harrison from their winter quarters in Virginia from a preacher that comes to visit us that has seen the boys. I will end this letter with a hope this war ends soon and we are together again.

Kiss the babes for me.

Your loving husband,
Schuyler

To change our routine, Harrison and I volunteered for burial duty. We walked over to the regimental hospital and about twenty dead were laid outside in rows for pick up and these men had died from wounds from the Fredericksburg battle. Due to the cold temperatures and the length of time since their deaths, the bodies were stiff as cordwood. When we began to lift the corpses into the wagon, I quietly said to Harrison, "The next time I volunteer for anything give me a quick kick." Harrison responded back quickly, "This aint to my liking neither."

Our work party took the bodies to an open field and with pick axe and muscle opened up twenty graves in frozen soil. It laid heavy on our thoughts that night as we hovered around our cabin fires. Here were men who were the same as us, no better, no worse. They stepped forward and their valor was called upon. When will we again hear the bugle's call as they did?

The last week of January brought our muster for pay, which was happily received. I've kept some of the money, but most of it gets sent home until I return. Another event worth a smile was receiving mail. But Harrison was the only member of our tent to get a letter which this time he shared with us.

Cone
Tuesday, January 20, 1863

Dear Harrison,

With pleasure I received your letter of the 17th instant. I am relieved that you and your brother are safe in Virginia.

Although you describe camp life during the winter as organized boredom, I was thoroughly intrigued. Picket duty certainly sounds eventful when you confront the enemy. Your telling of conversations while trading with the rebels sounds very exciting.

I can only imagine how uncomfortable it must be for you and the other brave men to spend so much time out in the cold and wet of winter. Please make sure you stay healthy and don't take any unnecessary chances.

Here at home, the school year progresses. Now that winter is in full season my class number have increased to twenty-five or thirty per day. One of my concerns has been dealing with the illnesses of my students. Winter has brought on colds and coughs and that means I'm missing usually half dozen pupils daily.

We have a large United States map on the wall and I have the older students point out where battles have taken place as we follow the news. We read about the tragic loss at Fredericksburg but we were glad that your regiment was spared.

Each morning I offer a prayer for the safe return of our brave soldiers and sailors.

I will be soon sending a box of surprises my students are making for you and Daniel and other local men. I hope you will enjoy them.

My parents send their prayers to you and Daniel and to Schuyler. Each Sabbath we sit by your family and enjoy their company.

I will end now but will write again soon. Please write back when you can.

Sincerely,
Katie

After hearing the letter I remarked to Harrison, "Brother, I still don't get how a nice, educated girl like that has any time for a shy, young farm boy like yourself. " As Harrison folds up the letter and puts it away in a canvas bag he slyly responds, "well boys, it aint no mystery to me, like you said, she's educated."

Also during the end of January, Lomira had responded to Schuyler's last letter with kind words of her own.

Paint Creek
Wednesday, January 22, 1863

My Dearest Schuyler,

I received your letter of the 14th instant with great happiness. I am much relieved that your injury continues to improve and I pray your full recovery is soon at hand.

The cane you described in your letter must be a true work of art. I cannot wait for the day I see you grasping it as you step of the train in Ypsilanti, home at last.

Elenora and Preston continue to ask when papa is coming home. I have occasionally reminded them that you and uncles Harrison and Daniel are on a long trip. Samantha, Thomas, and I try not to speak of the war in front of the young ones.

Harrison and Daniel wrote home stating that the regiment is in winter camp outside of Fredericksburg. Due to God's mercy the boys were not actively involved in the tragic battle in December. They seem to be in good health and spirits. They too pray for an end to this hateful war.

The winter here is tolerable. We haven't gotten a lot of snow. The path to the barn and chicken house can still be walked without plowing through drifts.

Thomas and John provided us with plenty of firewood and with the preserving Samantha and I did this fall, the children and I are getting by in fine style.

I am sending in a separate box the newspapers and other items you asked for. Plus you will find a few extra treasures from home.

We here at home read in the papers all the politics of this war, such as the President's recent proclamation about the slaves. In Michigan there are even some who are critical of the war. I don't pay much time to those kind. I know that you and your brothers are doing a righteous act in preserving our country.

I will end this letter now with my usual request that you listen to the doctors, take heed to what they say. I end each day listening to the young ones say their prayers and I add my own, my prayer for your safe return.

Love from your family,
Lomira

We had heard it more than once from Sergeant Maltman, that "to get mail you men need to write." That logic wasn't exactly new but we did go along and on a quiet Sunday, Harrison and I wrote to our parents and family what we've been up to.

A Soldier's Winter, November 1862–March 1863

Sunday, January 25, 1863

Dear John, Emma and Parents,

As I start to write this letter and put today's date, it came to me that we haven't been in this army six months yet but we've seen more than one war's worth of destruction and death.

Harrison and me are in tolerable health. We have built some huts for winter quarters. Our food is also fitting but our main task every day is to find firewood. When the sun rises at least one of us in every cabin goes looking for any wood we can find.

A few weeks back some of us in the company had the unpleasing task of burying the dead from the December battle. I and Harrison volunteered for one detail. We had to take around twenty dead from the hospital by ambulance to the burying field. Each body was wrapped in a blanket and layed in rows, heads to the North. I tell you folks Harrison agreed with me that it was one terrible job to do. I dare not describe the condition of the bodies were of these brave men. It truly will be a memory we won't long forget. We had to use pick axes to open the frozen ground.

Our regiment has gotten a fine reputation as being well disciplined and a strong fighting force.

Pay finally arrived last week. We were due pay back to November. Harrison and me will send most of it home. We keep some for buying at the sutler's store, which has few choices and high prices.

We have yet to see any effect from President Lincoln's emancipation act. Negroes can't get to lines thru the rebel pickets.

We hadn't got to see Schuyler at all for awhile but we did talk to a few guys who have returned to the regiment from being in the same hospital. They say they'd talked to him and he's mending well.

I Hear the Bugle's Call

We get our mail coming quicker now and would like to see more of it coming our way.

In our last letter I forgot to mention the morning of Christmas the Normal School boys and us farm boys sang some Christmas songs with Company E and some others as we had a little holiday celebration. A group of church people from the Christian Commission from Washington City came down with some cakes and pies and with the singing it seems almost like home, almost.

Brothers Harrison and Daniel
Company E
17th Michigan Vol Regiment
9th Corps
Falmouth, Virginia

To our surprise Sergeant Maltman's advice did prove correct. For early in February we received a very kind letter from our parents.

Cone, Michigan
Wednesday, February 4, 1863

Dear Daniel and Harrison,

We received your letter of the 25th ult with great happiness. Your Pa and I are quite relieved that your company was spared from the tragic battle that took place in December. Your description of the burial duty you boys shared fills us with a good amount of sorrow for those brave men and compassion for the families that will see their loved ones no more. We can only pray that the loss of such good men is due to providence.

John and Emma have been very helpful to Pa and me as we get older. The cold winters bring to us old folk the misery and John and Emma's support has been appreciated.

I know they have also looked in on Lomira and the children. They share news between what Lomira hears from Schuyler and what he hears from you boys.

In case you aren't up on news from Schuyler, he's mending well in the Maryland hospital. His leg is on the mend, but he don't know about his future in the Army. It would sure be blessing to us all if the Army would just send him home. Lomira and the rest of us could do a heap better job of nursing him back to health that those Army doctors can.

John tells us that your farm, Daniel, is surviving the winter in good shape.

There appears to be plenty of hay for the livestock to get by till spring. John checks on the house a few times a week and puts a fire going occasionally to warm the place and chase out any squirrels or coons that might have made home in the chimney.

Harrison, we have met that nice school teacher at Cone School, Katie Welch. She says she has written you a few times. I hope you've been a proper young man and have written her. She and her family are good Christians and we enjoy their company at the services.

I will end this now by saying that all of us back home are proud of the service you boys and others are rendering to our state and country. I know the Lord is watching over Schuyler and you boys.

Your loving parents,

P.S. Pa just told me to remind you boys to keep your heads down!

It was good to hear that they were doing well. I worry about our parents as they get on in age and hope their concern for us doesn't add to their woes. As I read the letter to Harrison, I stressed the motherly advice she had for him concerning Katie Welch by saying, "yes, proper young man, you do as your momma says." Harrison's throwing a dirty sock my way was his answer.

The month of February saw the Ninth Corps still in winter quarters in Virginia. Schuyler continued his recovery in the Frederick hospital and exchanging letters with Lomira.

I Hear the Bugle's Call

Frederick, Maryland
Wednesday, February 14, 1863

Dear Lomira and children,

As you probably can tell I'm writing this letter myself or trying to anyway. I hope you find my chicken scratches readable.

I was very happy to get your last letter of 22nd ult. My strength in my arms is about back to usual and I can now hold a pencil, at least for a few minutes at a time. I am real beholding to Mr. Cheever and Mr. Neumann for helping me these months I've been laid up.

My leg is still mending and the doctors seem pleased. No one is telling me when I can get out of here or where I'll go once I do skedaddle.

The Quaker girl, Rebekah, still comes around daily and we sometimes talk. It seems she knows the woodcarver that made my cane, his name is Thomas Keene. It seems he's made some furniture for the boarding house Rebekah and some other nurses stay.

I trust you are in good health and the Elenora and Preston are also. I can imagine how much they must be growing since I saw then in August. How I wish I was home now rocking them in my lap and enjoying the sight of you fixing our dinner.

When I can, I shuffle around the hospital and talk to other patients. As I see what shape some of the other men are in I swear I aint got no complaints. Some of the more recent patients arrived after the Fredericksburg battle. What they went through seems like no man should have to endure. Some of these men laid for a day or more huddled up under their dead friends waiting for either death or rescue. By the grace of the Almighty, they were saved. I hear that Harrison and Daniel and Company E escaped such a scene. I'm mighty relieved for that.

With winter comes a calm in this war but I fear what will arrive with the coming of spring.

The twinge in my hand has convinced me to end this letter. I hope your health is well as is the young one on the way. Please take care of yourself and pay my regards to Thomas and Samantha.

Kiss the babes for me
Schuyler

A Soldier's Winter, November 1862–March 1863

Paint Creek, Michigan
Wednesday, February 25, 1863

My Dear Schuyler,

With great happiness I received your letter of the 14th inst. Reading your letter and know it was written by you made my heart beat a bit faster. I am so happy you are gaining strength and I'm sure with the Lord's help will be fit as a fiddle soon.

Elenora and Preston are healthy and growing like weeds. Samantha has started to help me with the children's schooling as my condition starts to tire me some. Both of the young ones are getting along well with learning their numbers and practicing writing letters and words.

Samantha helps me with the winter house chores and Thomas makes sure we are taken care of and he also looks after the livestock.

John was over last week and mentioned that your parents remain in good health. Though your Pa has a touch of the misery but we know that at his years he suffers from that every winter. But of course being him, he won't admit to any ache or pain. Your Ma, as always has the right medicine for him, a pot of vegetable stew and a cup of her strong coffee.

Back here in Michigan the war news we read is mostly about how the South can't hold out much longer. Pastor Hoover has let some good discussions after Sabbath service. Anyone interested can stay after and share war news or opinions. I haven't stayed due to the late hour but Thomas usually does and he mentions that our community is still in support of President Lincoln and the righteous cause of this war.

The children ask me often about papa and I tell them that the trip you and Uncle Harrison and Daniel are on will be over soon. I do pray my answer to them comes true soon.

Thomas and Samantha mentioned to me to send along their best wishes and prayers for your recovery with this note.

I will end this with my prayer also for your recovery and safe return home.

Love from your children and Lomira

I Hear the Bugle's Call

We received a fine letter from Pastor Hoover. Getting mail from people not of our family really helps us feel that we aren't forgotten and our effort is respected.

Paint Creek, Michigan
Thursday, February 15, 1863

Dear Daniel and Harrison,

I pray that this letter finds both of you in good health and as safe as possible. Your family has kept the congregation and me informed of your heroic experiences. You boys and the others in Company E are constantly in our thoughts and prayers.

Lomira also keeps us aware of Schuyler's progress. We are pleased to learn of his steady progress and pray for his complete recovery.

Back here at home we continue to read of the battles and the rumors of peace. I am relieved that Company E was not heavily involved at Fredericksburg. Such a tragic loss of life on both sides of the battlefield.

The Ladies Aid Society is preparing another gift of winter clothes which we know you boys could put to good use.

Lomira and her children are doing fine and continue to have John and the others helping her on the farm.

I will end this letter by restating our pride in your service to our state, country and to the Lord.

In God's Name,
Pastor Neal Hoover

As the month was nearing its end Harrison and I wrote home.

A Soldier's Winter, November 1862–March 1863

February 20, 1863

Dear Parents and John and Emma,

Daniel and I really appreciated your letter of the 4th instant. Winter camp can get a good deal boring at times and reading a letter from home sure makes our day.

We wanted to let you know that our regiment has moved from outside Fredericksburg to a place called Aquia Creek. We didn't have to march through the ice and snow for we were put on railroad cars and given a ride. It seems this place we're now at is a large supply station. Me and Daniel aint seen so many wagons, guns, and horses since we been in this Army. So now of course we wonder why are we here? We don't hear nothing official but Daniel, James, and I figure we might be moving South come the spring. In January finally got back pay in "greenbacks." Payday doesn't come often enough.

Now that we've moved we don't have to draw picket duty no more. In place of picket duty we have plenty of drill. This drilling was necessary back when we were green but now us veterans don't hardly need it. At least it keeps us busy and moving around in this cold weather.

You folks probably read about General Burnside losing the command of the Army of the Potomac. We figure it was going to happen but we still think the general is a good man and hope he comes back to the Ninth Corps.

One of the last marches we went on was a good example of why armies don't fight in the winter. Last month our Regiment and most all the corps got called to formation. We weren't told why of course but rumor had it that we were gonna move on the rebel's flank. The weather had been miserable for days. We were getting more rain each day and the roads were mud bogs. We didn't move more than a few miles when we were told to backtrack to our camps. The wagons were up to the axles in mud and most of us had mud up to our knees. Even Captain Campbell expressed his opinion to a few of us by saying, "The Good lord must have wanted us to stay put this winter."

We are glad to hear the Schuyler's mending well. We had hoped to go up to see him but now that don't look possible.

We still share a tent with James Masters and we share our cooking fire with John Yaw and John Mason. Us Augusta boys take care of each other.

I Hear the Bugle's Call

We hope Ma and Pa and everyone else is in good health. We would sure look in favor if you folks could see your way to send us some dried fruit, coffee, canned goods and some socks.

We'll write when we know where we are off to.

>Harrison and Daniel
>Company E
>17th Michigan Volunteer Regiment
>Ninth Army Corps
>Aquia Landing, Virginia

The rumors of moving out started up as March began and with it the coming of spring. Spring would bring passable roads and fordable rivers, Harrison received a letter from Katie Welch which he did share with his tentmates, or most of it anyway.

>Cone
>
>Friday, March 6, 1863

Dear Harrison,

I was very pleased to hear again from you by your letter of the 14th ult. Camp life in winter time for you soldiers does sound rather routine after a while.

We read in the newspaper how the coming of spring may be the turning point in this war and you and the other brave men can come back home as victors. We pray that event happens soon.

Winter back here in Michigan is also a bit routine. My pa has been busy cutting timber and doing right well selling cordwood.

I've been busy at school with a full classroom until the last ten days in February we've seen the spread of mumps. One of Mr. Reinhold's boys came down first. In fact, Mr. Dennison, the district supervisor, has ordered our school closed for at least the next week. With so many students attending during the winter, any disease spreads quickly. Having had mumps myself as a child I'm not in its path. I do feel sorry for the afflicted and it does put a hold on our studies.

I continue to see your parents in church and do enjoy their company. And by the way, you still haven't mentioned how you liked the photograph I sent you. I do hope you received it.

I do enjoy your letters and I share your comments with my family (well most of your comments).

I will end this letter with a prayer for your safety and of your brothers.

                            Sincerely,

                            Katie

Schuyler and Lomira were keeping each other up to date and I found out later that John also began writing Schuyler.

                            Tuesday, March 10, 1863

My Dear Lomira and children,

I hope you can read this as my strength is getting better and I am now better able to hold a pencil. I really enjoyed your last letter and I sure wish I could be home seeing the young ones and of course you too. The doctors say I'm mending as I should be I do have my good days and my poor days. I blame the poor days on the weather. This here hospital is a big one and no amount of firewood keeps the stoves as warm as our parlor, that's for sure. The Quaker girl, Rebekah, continues to help me but I usually tell her to help the men who are worse off than me.

Last Sabbath a choir from the Methodist church came by and with the hospital chaplain, a first rate service took place. With my strength improving I've been able to move around more and help out the other patients when I can.

Lomira, tears would come to your eyes if you could see the suffering some poor souls have to bare with. There are times when I must walk away for I start to weep. But these men take their plight with an upstanding amount of

I Hear the Bugle's Call

strength of character and faith in the Lord.

I sure would like to hear from John. Let him know a letter from him and my parents would be welcomed. I pray that you continue to be in good health and do be careful. Do not stress yourself but call on Thomas or Samantha for aid. On the long winter nights my memory takes me back to our courtship days. I recall fondly sleigh rides after church and us doubling with John and Emma. And do you remember a few snowball fights? Ah, those were good days. We will have many more when this devilish business is over.

I must end now as I am needed to help a few men in my ward. Kiss the little ones for me.

Your loving husband,
Schuyler

Paint Creek
Thursday, March 19, 1863

My Dear Schuyler,

Thomas came from town with a special gift for me, a letter from you. I was so happy to not only hear how your health is improving but also seeing proof with your own handwriting.

Here, spring is slowly arriving. John and Thomas started tapping our maples and they tell me they've collected near 100 pounds of sugar so far. What we don't keep for us and the family Thomas will take over to Ypsilanti, Mr. Pennington, the dry goods owner, will buy all we can deliver.

I continue to enjoy good health but my, if you could see me you would certainly notice the appearance of a new babe on the way. I've told the children they will have a new brother or sister soon. They have started to think up names for the baby. I can't help but laugh at their name suggestions, they come up with the names of the pet goats or rabbits.

With the warmer spring weather the children are outside with Samantha which gives me some rest time.

John, Emma and your parents came by after church last Sabbath. They brought some fixins for dinner and we had a good meal. We certainly missed the other McFall menfolk. Your parents appear to be doing well. John and Emma are always there to help as well as your sisters.

I am very beholding to Rebekah and the other people who have looked after your care at the hospital. I'm sure my heart would break to see the suffering that many poor souls have to endure due to the wickedness of the South. You can be assured that we here at home are praying for an end to this evil war.

In your last letter you brought back cherished memories of an earlier time when we were young. I too have spent quiet times thinking of our courting days when our concerns were simpler and our dreams were many. But never fear my beloved, we will again share good times with each other and our precious children.

I do pray that your next letter brings news that not only of your improving health but that you will be on your way home soon. You've shown your bravery and devotion to our country, its time for another to take your place.

I'm sending another box of surprise items for you and perhaps a few extra to share if you choose.

My dear husband I must end this now for its late and a busy Friday is near.

Please take care and remember we are all thinking of you.

With deep affection,

Lomira and your babes

Paint Creek
Wednesday, March 25, 1863

Dear Brother Schuyler,

I am sure you are reading this with a look of surprise on your face. After all these months since you and our brothers went away a letter from me arrives. As you know I aint much for writing but Emma gave me the notion that I should keep up with my letter writing to my kinfolk.

I Hear the Bugle's Call

Lomira has kept us informed on your health and your improvement does ring as good news to us.

Emma has gone over to help Lomira as much as she can especially now as the new one is on the way. Samantha has been a great help to Lomira and children.

I thought you would like to be in on some of the local goings on. I've been busy tapping the maples on your farm and as well as Daniel's till he comes home.

Prices seem to keep rising. Wool could go for as much as 75 cents per pound this spring. I plan to sell a few of Pa's sheep after shearing. I've been offered 5 1/2 cents per pound. I'm hoping in a month or so to get my 6 cents or 7 cents per pound.

Last month I was offered 2 calves and a few pigs for my old bob sleigh by old man Day down near Stony Creek. I figured that was a deal made just for me. You remember how many times I had to fix up that sleigh?

Spring has started to arrive here in Paint Creek. This will be the first spring that you and Harrison and Daniel won't be here for the planting. But don't fret none. Thomas is a big help and Pa is still agile on his good days. We'll see to it that your place and Daniel's is started up in fine shape. We can only hope that this dreadful war will end soon so you boys can come home to work your land.

Everyone here is proud of what all of you are doing. And even though your laid up we have faith you'll be in first rate condition soon.

I'll end now as Emma tells me she sends her prayers for your complete recovery, as do all the family.

Brother John

Harrison and I agreed a letter from us to Schuyler should be done soon.

The rumors of our moving became fact during the middle of March. What our final destination would be was still unknown as we boarded the steamboat *Robert Morris*. During the next week two divisions of the Ninth Corps, which included our regiment rode train cars and steamboats, arriving in Cincinnati.

Louisville, Kentucky would be our final stop. In just over a week we did some serious traveling.

By early April we were still in Kentucky and about to look those rebels in the eye again. While settling in, I and Harrison did have the chance to write the family back home.

Tuesday, March 31, 1863

Dear Parents and Family,

While we have the chance Harrison and I wanted to let everyone back home know of our moving out of Virginia. Since our last letter a lot of events have gone on.

On the 17th of March our regiment boarded the steamboat *Robert Morris* for Baltimore. But due to a sudden snowstorm we couldn't land. We stayed on the boat for two days as a foot of snow fell. Seeing that storm surely reminded us a lot of spring snow back home in Michigan.

We finally got to walk on land and we were quickly put on railroad cars. The 17th was part of two divisions of the Ninth Corps moving west. Our train ride ended in a place called Parkersburg, Virginia. I can't say the town impressed us much. We then got on another boat called the *Majestic* with the Second Michigan and Seventy-Ninth New York.

On Wednesday the 25th we reached Cincinnati and got back on dry land. As I write this we just got to Louisville, Kentucky. Louisville is quite handsome, and looks like a thriving town. It strikes my liking more than most of these towns we've come through. We saw a large amount of bales of cotton back on the wharf at Parkersburg. We saw a steamer here at Louisville being crammed full when we got here. Harrison and me saw a large drove of mules, they were driving them like we do our cattle. I must admit the horses and mules here in Kentucky sure beat the ones we have back home.

We camped on the Preston farm—this man Preston was a U.S. Senator awhile back. We can buy provisions here. The boys trade their rations of meat, coffee and such for pies, cakes, eggs and other eatables. We was eight days on the march from our camp in Virginia. We figure we'd traveled about 1000 miles. The more I see of this state, the more I like it.

Some of us went to Sabbath service on Sunday night. The Chaplain spoke a fine sermon. We expect to get our next pay this week, about time too. We haven't got any mail since leaving Virginia. The wheat looks well along the river. Could be a good sign for the farms around here. So as you can see we've been doing a mess of traveling. Now what we going to here is up for discussion.

Of course the Generals and high officers don't tell us privates nothing so we just listen to the talk traveling through the camp. James Masters heard that we are supposed to go after rebel cavalry leader John Hunt Morgan. If that is so, we aint sure how us infantry are gonna catch up with men on horses.

Camp here in Kentucky is better than Virginia. Spring has seemed to arrive. We've noticed geese flying North and the streams are running ice free.

As you may have read, General Burnside was replaced by General Hooker and "Old Burnie" has come back to take over the Ninth Corps. We was pleased to see him come back to his old Corps.

Colonel Withington had to resign his command and go back home. It seems his infant daughter has died and his wife is serious ill. He spoke to us before he left about how proud he was to lead our regiment. He's a good man and we'll miss him. Colonel Luce has taken over the regiment.

Now that winter is ending I can see a pick up of spirit in the men. It was a long cold winter and we're anxious to get on and end this infernal war this year.

We hear that Schuyler is doing well and maybe me or Harrison will try to write him. Harrison and I are both in good health and hope everyone at home is as well.

We sure could use a few pair of socks and some of your good ginger-snaps, ma. Another month has almost gone, remember us to all. Notice our new mailing address.

>Your Sons,
>
>Harrison and Daniel
>Company E, 17th Mich Infantry
>1st Brigade
>1st Division
>Ninth Army Corps
>Cincinnati, Ohio

A Soldier's Winter, November 1862–March 1863

Spring in Kentucky is a pleasant sight. Wild flowers are starting to bloom, the wind is blowing kinder, and the sounds of songbirds are pleasant. But in the back of our thoughts is the cold realization that we still have a determined enemy to defeat, and for some good men, this kind and gentle spring will be their last.

WESTERN THEATER
IL
IN
MO
KY
WV
LOUISVILLE
VA
Siege of KNOXVILLE 11/17-12/4
CAMPBELL'S STATION 11/16
LENOIR STATION 11/15
NC
AR
TN
SC
MS
17th MICHIGAN VOLUNTEER INFANTRY REGIMENT ATTACHED to the ARMY of the OHIO & ARMY of the TENNESSEE ~IN THE WEST~
Siege of VICKSBURG 6/14-7/4
LA
JACKSON 7/10-17
AL
GA
FL
1863

On the Move
April 1863 – June 1863

With spring now appearing each day in its uniform of warmer winds and brighter colors our camp took on a more hospitable appearance as each company cleaned up the refuse of winter. On an early evening in April I took pencil in hand and wrote to Brother John.

Thursday, April 2, 1863

Dear Brother John and Emma,

Harrison and I have been on the move quite a bit lately. As I write this our regiment is camped near Louisville, Kentucky. How we got here is a long story which I described in my last letter to Ma and Pa.

The reason we was sent west was to help track down some rebels led by Morgan. Two divisions of the Ninth Corps were sent west. We don't mind being here in Kentucky. It looks like spring is about started and that's fine with us. I wanted to ask how my farm has been doing this winter? Any new calves? What are the market prices for spring wool? How'd the livestock come through the winter? I trust the maple sap has begun to run. How I miss being home in the spring and working in my woods. I am much thankful for your taking on my farm as I know you and Emma have a pile of other chores to look over. Harrison and I also thank you two for keeping watch over Pa, Ma, and the girls.

You might be interested in what we pay for some goods. We have a person called a sutler who is licensed to sell general goods to the soldiers. Usually the prices are fair but it seems he knows when to raise his prices. Recently he charged us 5 cents an apple, 50 cents for honey, 50 cents for cheese and

I Hear the Bugle's Call

85 cents for butter. And of course some paid these ridiculous prices cause of army supplies being late. But Harrison, James, and I refused to be bamboozled. Before we left Virginia we heard Schuyler was healing well. We would like to see him return to our company but maybe it would be best for him and Lomira if he was sent home.

Some of us venture into the country when we can. We stop by the homes and farms and get meals. We then get to talk with the people. Some pretend to be Union but later their slaves say they are "right smart" rebels. The President's proclamation is not wanted here.

We do hope the coming of spring brings the end to this war. We have seen far too many good men lost defending our just cause.
Please share our words with friends and family.

                        Sincerely,

                        Harrison and Daniel
                        Company E, 17th Mich Infantry
                        1st Brigade
                        1st Division
                        9th Army Corps
                        Cincinnati, Ohio

And Schuyler and his beloved Lomira kept up their spirits by exchanging letters.

On the Move

Saturday
April 4, 1863

My Dear Lomira and Children,

As I hope you can see my handwriting is getting better as the days go by. I was much pleased getting your last letter. I sure wish I was home tapping those maples myself. I am much beholden to Thomas and John for helping out. You probably know that John sent me a fine letter just a while ago. It was good to hear from him and it caught up on local news.

I trust you've been takin care of yourself as I guess the new arrival aint far away. You make sure Samantha is nearby to help you through your days.

My leg continues to heal and I can walk pretty much without the cane. I do confess that I aint near in shape to plow any fields yet, but that'll come.

The doctors are saying I might be transferred to another hospital over in Ohio. If so, that leads me to believe that I aint going back to Company E no time soon. I guess that's good news, but I do miss not being with my brothers and doing my part in this war.

As spring has begun here in Maryland the tree blossoms and warmer winds do remind me of spring back home. I do wish to come home to be with you and the little ones. Maybe soon we can be together.

I'm about out of stamps and writing paper. Also, any pipe tobacco you can send would be most appreciated. Kiss the babes for me.

Your loving husband
Schuyler

We also found the time to write to our brother Schuyler.

I Hear the Bugle's Call

Wednesday, April 8, 1863

Dear Schuyler,

Harrison and I we've been guilty of not writing to you and filling you in on what Company E has been doing.

As you might know, our regiment has been sent west to Kentucky. General Burnside has come back to command and we moved west last month.

Right now we are near Louisville and our job is to chase General Morgan and his cavalry. How us foot soldiers are going to catch horse soldiers, they aint told us yet. We seen some first rate country here in Kentucky. Spring has started and we seen peach trees and others in bloom. Most of the farms are small and only seen a few slaves. What is happening is that after the President's proclamation a whole lot or runaways have come in. This has made most of the Sesesh folk around here spittin mad at any blue coats in the area. Colonel Withington resigned his command last month. His daughter died and his wife is seriously ill too. We were sad to see him go. You know, he is a good man. Colonel Luce has taken his place. So far he's been an acceptable replacement.

We hear from John that you are mending and that's good news. James Masters and Theron Stevens send their good words. We all agreed that our fireside talks aint been as enjoyable since your departure. We'd like to see you back but we know Lomira surely would like you home too.

We hope your hospital food aint as bad as our army victuals. But here in Kentucky we have been able to buy some vegetables, milk, bread and a few hogs and chickens have come over to our side.

We'll be ending now as we hear the bugle's call. Take care of yourself.

Daniel and Harrison

> Company E, 17th Michigan Infantry
> 1st Brigade
> 1st Division
> 9th Army Corps
> Army of the Ohio
> Cincinnati, Ohio

As we found out later, Pastor Hoover also sent his prayers and well wishes to Schuyler.

> Paint Creek
> Wednesday, April 8, 1863

Dear Schuyler,

I do apologize for not writing you previous to this letter. Lomira has kept the congregation and me aware of your condition. And we praise the Almighty for your steady recovery.

Lomira mentions that you have received the best of care and we are glad to hear it is so.

Our congregation continues to support all our brave men and we share the grief of the families that have lost loved ones.

Your brother John passes along news of Harrison and Daniel, James Masters, and the other Augusta men.

The newspapers here at home talk of peace rumors but after two long years we are never sure.

The Ladies Aid Society continues to sew and knit items for the men and I know they plan on sending you and others a package of clothing and edibles soon.

Lomira and the children are doing well in your absence but of course wish you were here as we all do.

I Hear the Bugle's Call

I will close with a reminder to you to trust in the Lord and he will bring you home safely.

In God's Name,
Pastor Neal Hoover

Our daily routine in Kentucky began with reveille. Breakfast was then made by a group of tentmates. We then had guard mounting at 9 a.m. followed by company drill. After noon meal came battalion drill of one to two hours. Dress parade usually took place around 5 p.m. Later in the evening was roll call and tattoo. One of the days favored by most was wash day. Of course a clean water supply was helpful, but not always available. And by wash day I mean clothes and humans getting a much needed scrub down.
Lomira continued to update Schuyler on news from home.

Paint Creek
Tuesday, April 14, 1863

Dear Schuyler,

I happily received your letter of the 4th inst. and I certainly can see a stronger hand on the pencil. Your continued improvement is God's will.

Thomas and Samantha are greatly interested in your recovery and ask about you constantly.

John and Thomas have been pulling some old stumps near the creek and they tell me to let you know its about sheep shearing time.

As the time of our newborn is near I find I look forward to sitting more than standing over a hot stove. Samantha has been a heaven sent and even the children have taking up some of the smaller chores. I do believe I'll be in fine health for the arrival next month. I know I mustn't, but I do wish you would be home when that day comes.

Your Pa and John stopped by two days ago as they were coming back from Ypsilanti. Pa appears right healthy and says your ma is making up a box of home treats to be sending you.

The war news he hears talks of activity starting in Virginia now that General Hooker commands that Army of the Potomac. As you may know the 17th has moved west to Kentucky under General Burnside. It appears your brothers sent word to John that two divisions were sent to Kentucky as rebel forces are raising a ruckus. They told John they expect to stay there in the south for awhile. If you feel up to it, why not write them a letter?

As spring starts to appear here, I really can't help but think back to past years with you working the fields and I doing my spring cleaning. Those good days will again return and with our new babe to add to our family, we are blessed.

I must now end as its time to hear the little ones' prayers and put them to bed.

                        With love from your children and me,
                        Lomira

As the days of April continued on their march a most interesting event took place. On a particularly drab Wednesday we heard Sergeant Maltman shout out some of the words most cherished, "mail call!" With that announcement a swarm of eager soldiers encircled the sergeant like bees around the hive. Although my luck ran bad that day, Harrison received a letter that he seemed most happy to accept. He chose not to share it with me or anyone else.

                        Cone
                        Thursday, April 16, 1863

Dear Harrison,

I was so pleased to get your letter of the 30th ult. We had heard that the Seventeenth Michigan might be moving south. Now I see you and your brother are just a few states from us.

I thank you for the letter you sent the school. My students follow the war news quite closely and six of them have fathers or brothers in the army. My older boys are all saying they want to join up and although they aren't of age, they still talk of finding their way in after the school year is over. I do not see them as soldiers, but young boys. I can't see them living the life as soldiers as you have described it.

Your telling of army life has been followed intently by the class. We have used your regiment's moves as geography lessons. We have also learned about the different region's weather and economy. I want the class to learn from the war as much as they can.

On a more personal note, your letters continue to bring me pleasure as they occupy my mind away from the tasks at the schoolhouse. Even my father asks about you. You asked about a lock of my hair. I will agree to such a request only if you supply the same to me. Enclosed, you will find my contribution to our agreement.

Finally spring has arrived and the spring chores have taken away about half of my students. So, for about the next ten days my class consists of the younger ones.

That's fine because I can now give them more attention. I'm not sure what I will do during the summer months. My contract does allow me to work outside the school year, but doing only appropriate tasks.
I will close now as I prepare for Friday's lesson. Please write when you can and take care of yourself.

Sincerely,
Katie

I and James Masters watched him closely as he read each line silently. "Harrison," I asked, "who could be sending you a letter of such interest?" I winked at James and continued, "It couldn't be a young schoolteacher from Cone now could it?"

Harrison said nothing at first but folded up the letter back in the envelope and started out of the tent. James quickly asked, "Where you off to?" Harrison rather sheepishly replied, "I'm gonna look up Theron Stevens, I could use a haircut."

My luck on mail day did turn toward the better a few weeks later.

> Paint Creek
> Thursday, April 30, 1863

Dear Brothers,

Emma and me was pleased to read your last letter. Now that you boys are in the west we may read more about your regiment in the newspapers. Most of the war news from back east aint so good. Back here in Michigan some of those so called Peace Democrats are spouting off in the newspapers. Of course, these men aint been close enough to war to hear a rifle shot. Most of the men here back in the area don't pay those big mouths no mind.

We also hear from Schuyler that he is mending fine. He still aint heard about what he's gonna do but we all here hope he comes home. Lomira is near having the baby and having Schuyler home would ease her mind greatly.

Daniel, now with spring coming on your orchard is looking good. Pa, Thomas, and me have been washing the sheep and we're about to commence shearing.

Thomas and me have begun our plowing. We started on some of Schuyler's land. We then will move over to your land Daniel, then to mine and Pa's. We bought a second team of horses, we got a good deal from Mr. Bunton. So with two teams working and good weather, our task should go a might quicker.

Our maple trees produced well over 100 pounds of sugar and we got a good price in Ypsilanti.

I'll be stopping for now and take up the pen again soon. Emma sends her best and Ma and our sisters do too. I can't say "Ma don't worry none," but she knows you boys are in God's care. We'll be looking forward to hearing from you two again.

Brother John

It was good to hear that the routine of spring chores was commencing back home. Harrison and I both agreed knowing that as life back home continued at its normal pace, we would one day end our routine of the soldier's life and return with pleasure to the work of the farm.

Furloughs for us enlisted men were few and far between. But in early May three men from Company E did get to go home to do some recruiting. The Army doesn't allow a man to go home just because he wants to. Some of the men who have come back from furlough report that they saw no effects of the war at home except higher prices for crops and livestock. And it seems to many people back home have very little sense as to what we in uniform have to put up with.

We have heard that Jackson, Mississippi had been taken by our forces and burned. If true this tightens the noose around Vicksburg. Rumors in camp say we're off to help Grant take that city and finally control all of the Mississippi River. As the month of May marched on, I and Harrison wrote home.

Wednesday, May 20, 1863

Dear Pa, Ma and family,

Here we are still in Kentucky, we've been marching from one side of the state to the other. As I write this our regiment is near Jamestown.

We do not see much of the enemy except for a cavalry patrol, or we catch a sleeping rebel on picket duty.

On the Move

Most of our camp routine still is drill, drill, and more drill. We noticed here in Kentucky the President's proclamation carries some weight. Even though it doesn't have no legal hold on this border state. Just about every day some runaway slave makes it into our lines. They are most happy to see us "Lincoln men" as they call us. Some have sad and frightening tales of their escape. They also tell of the ones they know don't get away.

Spring here in the South is right pleasing with blossoms appearing on the trees and the clover is near ready for cutting.

But as I and Harrison look back on the time we've spent in the army we both agree one change we noticed is how we view death. Back home when a friend dies we are saddened by their passing. Since we've taken on the uniform we have seen men of both armies in death's repose. We have seen scenes of death we wish to never recall. We have become so accustomed to the effects of shot and shell we walk on as death has become as routine as cleaning our rifles. This different view was not possible a year ago, another part of this war we didn't bargain for.

We hear we may be moving to Tennessee soon. Our regiment may go to help General Rosecrans clean out the rebels down there.

Harrison and I will end now as I hear the bugle's call for assembly.

> Your loving sons,
> Daniel and Harrison
> Company E
> 17th Michigan Vol Reg
> 1st Brigade
> 1st Division
> 9th Corps
> Army of the Ohio
> Cincinnati Ohio

Lomira and Schuyler were sharing important news of their own.

I Hear the Bugle's Call

Paint Creek
Friday, May 29, 1863

Dear Schuyler,

I have joyous news to tell you today! Our blessed event has taken place! The Lord has given us a fine, healthy boy to add to the McFall clan! The birth took place two days ago on May 27th.

You may notice the handwriting of this letter looks different. Samantha has kindly written this as I am a bit tired from my recent "activity." Do not fear as I am in good health. Samantha helped with the birth and Dr. Kelly came not long after. Thomas had gone to Paint Creek to fetch him when the signs began.

We now must choose a name. Elenora and Preston are fascinated with their new brother but they aren't pleased with his cries. I asked them for their ideas for a name but naming him for their goat wasn't my choice.

I anxiously await your choice. As you can see I have one more reason for your recovery and return home.

I'll write again as I am able to. Please take care.

Your loving family,
Lomira and babes
Friday, June 12, 1863

Dear Lomira,

I just got your letter of the 29th ult. I couldn't be more happy to hear of our new son. That news has been the best medicine I have gotten since I was wounded. I am really beholding to Samantha and Dr. Kelly for taking care of your and our son. I am also pleased to hear your feeling healthy as is the baby.

I have some news for you to. Since my last letter I've been transferred. First, I was sent to a hospital in Cincinnati, Ohio. Now for about a week I'm at Camp Dennison outside of Cincinnati. The doctors are telling me that I may be getting a medical discharge. The Army has to decide if I am healthy enough for the Invalid Corps. That's a group of soldiers that got wounded who are too bad off to fight, but tolerable for other duties. They told me I'll hear their idea soon enough. My leg has healed mostly, but I do have a limp and don't get around too rapid. I will write as soon as I know what they decide.

As to a name for our son, I kinda favor the name Perry. I got to know a doctor by that name back in Frederick and he was a good man.
When you write, notice my new address. Kiss all three babes for me.

                                           Your loving husband,
                                           Schuyler
                                           Camp Dennison
                                           Cincinnati, Ohio

And Schuyler also wrote a letter to John which John kept as a secret from the family.

I Hear the Bugle's Call

>   Saturday
>   June 13, 1863

Dear Brother John,

As I am still here at the hospital in Ohio I wanted to pass along my memories of what happened to me in the early days after my wounding last fall. I've been having some nights when I wake up in a cold sweat and I think I'm charging the rebels again. The doctors here say what's happening to me is common for soldiers but that don't make it easier. They say if I talk about those days back then my mind might be calmed.

I thought I would write you cause you're better to understand and I don't want Lomira or our parents to fret none. I trust you will agree with my notion.
On that afternoon of the battle our company had crossed over the bridge that our regiment had been tussling with rebels for since early in the afternoon.

Harrison, Daniel and I with Company E started towards Sharpsburg. We hadn't got more than a few hundred rods when we were hit by artillery and rifle fire. We were moving at the quick step when I heard an explosion and saw a cloud of dirt explode to my side. I then felt a burning feeling near my left knee, which caused my leg to buckle, and I went down like a chopped elm. I was awake enough to see my left leg was soaked in red. Strange as it may sound, it took me a bit of time to come to the notion that what I was seeing was my blood. Daniel and Harrison weren't hit and came by me quickly. Daniel gave me his canteen and I then laid low waiting for help. I must have fainted there after cause when I come to I notice I'm lying on the ground in a tent. What strikes me first is the sounds. I'm hearing men screaming in pain. Some calling out for loved ones, others begging for water, anything to end their pain. A doctor comes over to me and inspects my wound. He must have seen the question in my face for he assures me that my leg aint needed to come off. As he started to clean and dress the wound I must of blacked out again for the next time I'm awake I'm laying in an ambulance wagon being tormented as the wagon's wheels hit every rut and rock along the route. As I raise my head I see I'm sharing this ride with three other men. Riding in the wagon is a young man who is looking after all of us. My wound has been bandaged but the pain is beyond description. I asked the attendant for something to ease my trouble but he said I'd have to wait till I got to the field hospital. A few sips of water did ease me some.

We arrived at a barn which had become a hospital. And at that place I truly was horrified. I could see outside a pile of what looked like cordwood. But it didn't take long to see I was sadly mistaken. For as I was watching while laying on a pile of straw I saw men with bloody aprons and boots the color of red dropping not wood in the pile but arms and legs that had been cut off. I must confess this sight and the stench hanging over this place did make my stomach churn.

My wound wasn't judged as severe as many others and for that I was lucky. The pain was severe and I know my voice was added to the chorus of sufferers that seemed to echo off the barn walls. Sometime later, a surgeon came and looked at my wound, I was then carried over to a wood door used as a surgeon's table. A nurse then put a cloth filled with something over my face and I must have fallen asleep.

When I came to I noticed it had become nightfall and I was laying outside looking at the stars. Being groggy, I had a devil of a time figuring out where I was. A nurse came by checking on me and told me I had gone through the surgery well though they took a bunch of metal my leg was saved. She did say how good the healing would be. She said I'd be sent to a larger hospital back in Frederick, Maryland to rest up and finish healing. Only then would I know if I could get back with my company or not. As much as I would like to go home to Lomira and the children, I felt my job wasn't done yet. I had to go back and march on with Daniel and Harrison.

As you know I've stayed at the Frederick hospital for months. And no one here is telling me yet what's to become of me, so I wait.

During my stay here I've talked to many a man who has gone through the storm like me. In fact, from I'd seen, I'm better off than most of the poor souls here. We all have suffered, we all endure pain, and we all have had bad dreams of death and battle. I pray that these memories that at times have scared the devil out of me will end.

I do have a heap of gratitude for the men and women who was there to help me and the other men. They put their lives up for us working so close to the battle. They are as brave as the men who have fallen.

I needed to share these torments with someone who I felt would understand. I trust you will look kindly toward me for doing so.

Brother Schuyler
Camp Dennison
Cincinnati, Ohio

The month of June was certainly a time for men on the move. By the third week in the month our Regiment was in Mississippi close enough to Vicksburg to hear the artillery thundering away. This constant barrage consists of artillery rounds of 20 to 30 per hour.

We've hear rumors that General Lee has invaded Maryland again and is on the old South Mountain battlefield. General Hooker and the Army of the Potomac is on the rebel's tail. I hope this time General Lee and company are finally trapped and then this war may soon be over.

During the quiet of a few hours of our artillery at rest I penned a letter home to Brother John and wife, Emma.

On the Move

Saturday, June 20, 1863

Dear John and Emma,

As I write this Harrison and I are down here in Mississippi and to say the least we are on the move. This since our last letter home our division went by rail to Lebanon then Louisville, then ferried the Ohio River. We then boarded freight cars to Seymore, Indiana. Finally after changing cars at Sandoral, Illinois got to Cairo about midnight.

We passed through some fine country. We were greeted at every stop by townspeople cheering us on. It seemed like at every town we were welcomed with people waving handkerchiefs, serving us pies, cakes and coffee.
We got to Washington, Indiana about midnight as we were all sleeping. But we were awakened not by a gruff sounding sergeant, but young ladies opening up the freight doors calling to us. "Soldiers—get up and get something to eat. We want to see you brave men. We've come a ways to see you and bring you something to eat." Awakening to such a call I and Harrison both agreed we must be dreaming. But to our surprise, it was truly happening.

At Cairo we boarded the steamer Lenora and reached Memphis, Tennessee early Monday morning. Along the river ride rebel guerillas fired from the shoreline but no harm done. Early in the morning on Thursday we got to a place called Haines Bluff, it's near the Yazoo River. We aint far from Vicksburg, which I suppose is a place you heard about.

Down this far south we seen many cotton plantations, some still standing, but most a pile of ashes. Our regiment is here if needed for the taking of Vicksburg. We are in the overall command of General Grant.

We've done some serious marching and we are all worn to a frazzle.

We are close enough to hear the artillery shelling Vicksburg. This morning we heard what sounded like a thunderstorm off in the distance. We were told by Sergeant Maltman it was man-made thunder.

The weather down here has been right pleasant. When not on picket duty we've had the time to go scouting for anything to fill our stomachs. We've come across quite a bit of berries, apples, and such.

Foraging teams have brought in a good number of cattle, horses, and mules claimed from rebel farms. We also see more negroes coming into our lines as they decide to run away from their owners. Back home, we seldom used to talk about slavery; it just didn't mean much. But down here slavery slaps you in the face. To see the condition of some of these poor souls or hear their tales would bring a tear to the eye of any God fearing man.

We've been joined by two Michigan regiments, the Twelfth and Fifteenth. Also, we have started to wear a Ninth Corps patch. A few months back General Hooker authorized each corps to wear a different style patch. Our patch is a shield made of wool. It looks right smart on our caps.

I almost forgot to mention what happened to me awhile back. I got promoted to Corporal earlier this month. I didn't even know I was up for it. Captain Campbell called me over to this tent. I figured I was going to get spoken to for some army infraction I didn't follow. But to my surprise he commenced to read me the order from Colonel Luce promoting me. I was near to falling over when he told me. Harrison and the other men back in my tent were near surprised as me. With this promotion comes a five dollar a month raise and some extra duties.

I'll be ending this now as a real rainstorm is heading our way and Harrison and I need to help store our equipment.

Tell everyone we are doing fine and will write again soon.

Harrison and Daniel
Company E
1st Brigade
1st Division
Ninth Corps
Army of the Tennessee

Lomira continued to write to Schuyler of news and moral support.

>Paint Creek,
>Monday, June 21, 1863

Dear Husband,

I received your letter from the 12th inst. and I am excited to hear that you are now in Ohio. I can only hope and pray that your transfer means you will be on your way back here to Michigan soon.

Because you are a patriotic and good man, should you be sent home, I know your dedication to duty would call on you to stay and fight on. The cause that took you and your brothers from us is a noble and just one. I of course would be most happy to see you come home, but only if the army says it's the right decision.

Your suggestion concerning the name of our new son is an excellent one. Perry is a good name and is a good pairing with his brother. Both Preston and Elenora are taken with their new brother. But they don't know why he chooses to cry when he does.

Samantha has been a saint as I regain my strength and Emma has been a God-sent also.

I'll await Perry's baptism until I hear more from you about when we should have it done and who would be the Godparents.

I will end this letter sending you all the love of your family and hope to hear from you soon. Do heed the doctor's advice and take care of yourself.

>Your loving family,
>Lomira

As June was ending it appeared to Harrison and me that with Vicksburg would surely be in our hands soon, the war here in the West may be coming to a crucial stage. If we gain control of all the Mississippi River we cut the rebel country in two. If General Hooker can whip the rebs in Maryland then maybe this infernal war ends this summer and the killing stops. But I still cannot forget the look of the rebels we meet and their fiery resolve not to accept defeat.

As Harrison and I look back to almost a year in this war, we have seen too many good men given their lives for our country's cause. We have not been beaten by the enemy and with God's will, will not see defeat. But there is a look of the men I see, and perhaps visible in my eyes also. The look is not of fear, not of giving up, but of exhaustion. There is exhaustion in a war that has gone on for two long years and the destruction of lives, hopes, and dreams. We will continue to perform our duty but this dreadful storm of war must end soon.

On the Move

I Hear the Bugle's Call

"We Are All The Same"
July 1863 – September 1863

As July came upon the calendar and our nation's day of Independence, Schuyler sent a letter of his thoughts from his new location in Ohio to his beloved Lomira.

Saturday, July 4, 1863

Dear Lomira and children,

I was much pleased to get your letter of the 21st ult.. I am much, and your letters still are the best medicine for me.

The hospital here is much larger than in Maryland and it seems the patients are like me—there are more walking wounded than bedridden. But the doctors here are akin to those in Maryland, they don't tell a person nothing. I keep asking if I will go back to the regiment, all they say is, "its not been determined yet."

I'm able to get around with a cane and I try to help with the other patients when I can. Time goes by faster when I keep myself busy. The food is first rate and I might even put on a pound or two during my stay here.

I do hope your keeping in good health. I pray also, our youngest baby is doing well as well as Preston and Elenora. I agree, we can wait awhile on Perry's baptism. I would believe Pastor Hoover won't mind us waiting awhile.

I heard from Daniel and Harrison and they brought me up to date on what's happening with the company and the regiment. I wish I was with them as they face the enemy. There are times I feel like I failed at my duty. This confounded wound has kept me from doing what I signed up to do, serve as my brothers are doing. But I guess a plan for me is still to be determined.

I Hear the Bugle's Call

I will end now as a celebration is planned for us here as we celebrate our country's day of freedom. Kiss all three babes for me.

>With love,
>
>Schuyler
>
>Camp Dennison
>Cincinnati, Ohio

For the Seventeenth Michigan early July found us outside of Vicksburg, Mississippi. General Grant's siege of that river fortress had gone on for weeks. The 17th was not directly involved as we were there in case Rebel General Johnston, had tried to relieve the encircled town from the East.

As the Fourth of July neared, the Union artillery barrage continued. It was as if the sky was exploding.

On the afternoon of the third, Harrison, James Masters, and John Yaw and I began an adventure that we will never forget.

Early after noon meal last Friday Sergeant Maltman called, "Corporal McFall, select three men and come with me!" Not knowing what was at hand I "volunteered" Harrison, James Masters and John Yaw to follow me to the sergeant's tent. My three mates asked me what was going on and, as I didn't know either I just said, "Sergeant wants us on the quick step."

As we approached, Sergeant Maltman was talking with Captain Campbell. So, we hung back until called for. We saw the Sergeant nod in agreement and offer the appropriate salute. He walks over to us and says, "Corporal have your men fill your cartridge pouches, fill canteens, pick up your rifles and meet me here at my tent after tattoo tonight."

The sergeant was more secretive than usual which gave us all the notion that wherever we're going we might not like it.

So as tattoo sounded I and the others picked up our accoutrements and muskets, which also included some pork, hardtack, coffee, a blanket and a couple of rope bridles, which Sergeant Maltman ordered us to bring along.

As we got to the camp perimeter, the sergeant said softly but sternly, "Men, from here on out no talking, no whistling, stay together and no turning back." Hearing those commands made all of us look at each other in the dim light with looks of uneasiness.

We all nod our understanding of our orders and begin the march to who knows where? Though we weren't told where we were going, we could pick up on our own, we were headed toward the thunder in the distance—Vicksburg.

As we began our procession Sergeant Maltman stopped us a few rods outside of camp and in a hushed voice said, "Men, we are going on a mission first to find animals to fill these bridles, then hopefully ride not walk to Vicksburg."

He surely sensed our surprise when he added, "We have gotten permission from Colonel Luce down to Captain Campbell to go sightseeing." He went on telling us that the commanders from Regiment and up believe the fight is over and in fact within a day or two may come the surrender. He added, " It would be quite the experience if some of the company could take a look at what's been the Federal target for months. And I thought you boys might want to be the storytellers back in camp." We each nodded in agreement and continued our travels with an increased sense of interest.

We knew that our camp was about fifteen miles from the Vicksburg defense perimeter so we hoped our luck would be with us as we scoured the area along the road for horses or mules so as to save shoe leather.

It was commonly known by soldiers that the first man to come across a horse or mule, could claim and bridle it. This acquisition was his until the quartermaster claimed it.

Our search was somewhat successful as we came across an old plow horse. A horse barely standing is better than none at all so we claimed our war prize and took turns riding and walking. Harrison made the remark after a few miles, "Boys, I don't think this here creature will get us a ribbon at the county fair, but it does beat walking."

About half way we stopped by an old work shed and rested awhile. We awoke after a few hours had passed and the first rays of daylight could be seen in the east.

After a quick meal of coffee, pork and hard tack we began our travel arriving at the Union perimeter after 8 a.m. Here was a most unusual sight. The Union men were mostly engaged at preparing their breakfast and not more than a few rods distance were the rebels sitting on the banks of their trenches. White flags were evident sticking in mounds of dirt on both sides.

We were told that there had been no fighting there for a day and the guns we had heard were our artillery in salute. The story that was circulating was that Confederate General Pemberton had offered to surrender in the last day or two but General Grant would not accept anything but unconditional surrender.

As we came up to an open area of the line we saw a gathering of uniforms. We asked a bystander what was going on and he pointed to a tree aways off and there stood a rebel Colonel who was soon met by three Union officers. We were only a handful of rods from the whole event.

Papers were exchanged between the rebels and Grant's staff and off the Union officers went. We continued walking along the line as we came across small groups of rebels and our men. The rebels said they were all for surrender for they were terrible hungry. They were anxious to trade most any possessions of theirs for hard tack or bacon. We were a little nervous about mixing with the enemy, but our curiosity won out and Sergeant Maltman suggested we follow him to the city.

We got to the river as a big gunboat appears which we later learned was Admiral Porter's flagship called Black Hawk. It was quite a sight to behold as it had three rows of portholes and six or eight pieces of artillery. The Marines on board were dressed in white pants, white shirts with blue collars, and hats with wide black ribbons. The officers were draped with gold lace.

The rebel prisoners we came across were unsure as to their fate. To a man they spoke of wanting nothing more of this war. "Just parole us and we will skedaddle home, no more fighting for us," was spoke by most we talked to.

After walking around town awhile we found an old shed which contained a useable stove. We made a dinner from what we packed, and ate in Vicksburg on the Fourth of July. This is one Fourth celebration we all will remember for the rest of our lives.

About sundown we commenced to getting back to camp. When we returned to camp we had quite a story to tell our comrades.

What I saw of the rebel soldiers living conditions and their appearance was a shock. We heard stories of how soldiers and civilians including women and children lived in caves burrowed like moles to survive. But to see the real thing, to walk among the destruction of property and life was truly a glimpse into the tragedy of war. I don't think I'll ever forget the sight of two small lads of four or five years clinging to the mama out of fear, shaking for want of food. The leaders of the South brought this on their own people. The suffering taking place must end soon. Whether we are a frightened lad of five, a soldier with a rifle, or a President, in God's eyes, we are all the same.

On the morning of the fifth of July we received orders to pack our equipment as we headed east towards the state capital at Jackson. We commenced a slow march foraging as we went along. We camped early one night which allowed me time to pen a letter home to our parents.

> Tuesday, July 7, 1863
> Near Jackson, Mississippi

Dear Ma and Pa and sisters,

As I write this letter Harrison and I are in Mississippi not far from the Vicksburg battlefield. And we have a tale to tell everyone.

As you may have heard by the time you get this letter, the siege of Vicksburg has ended and the rebels have surrendered to Grant on the Fourth of July.

To top off that news Harrison, James Masters, Sergeant Maltman and me were at the battlefront and seen the surrender take place.

As the artillery battle had stopped on the third we heard that the rebels were about done in and ready to give up.

I Hear the Bugle's Call

Sergeant Maltman got a pass from Lieutenant Safford permitting me, Harrison, James Masters, John Yaw, and the Sergeant, to go to the city. After tattoo on Friday night the third of July we packed up a few rations, a blanket, and a couple of bridles. Only after we got to the camp perimeter did he tell us where we were going. We traveled about fifteen miles while riding on an old plow horse we found along the way.

I'll wrap up the adventure by saying that we got up to the front and lo and behold we come across the rebel commander and Grant's staff officers handing over what we learned later were surrender demands to the rebels.

Later we came across some of our men and rebels talking and our men were sharing their rations. The Southern boys did look in pitiful shape and the clothes looked as rags.

Our squad returned to our company shortly thereafter with quite a story to tell. After seeing the condition of our enemy it surely seems cruel to continue this war. The rebels need to face facts and stop this infernal conflict.

I'll end now as it appears our regiment is about to take Jackson by attack or siege. Our hope is that each town, each village we take from the rebels leads to a quicker end to this war.

Hope everyone is fine. You folks don't need to worry none, we are keeping ourselves in fine shape.

                        Harrison and Daniel,

                        Company E
                        1st Brigade
                        1st Division
                        9th Corps
                        Army of the Tennessee

For about a week we laid siege to Jackson until they surrendered for fear of their city being totally destroyed.

What came next was a departure from our normal duties. We spent about three days tearing up the rebel's railroad lines of the Mississippi Central Railroad. As Corporal, I was ordered to take some men and begin ripping up track. Another group began a huge fire of logs and track ties. We then placed a few rails at a time in the fire. After a time we dragged them out and twisted them around a few large tree trunks. We knew by doing this the rebels aint about to put these back to use again. As July went by we did see our mail catch up to us which eased our minds.

I received a fine letter from Pastor Hoover

> Friday, July 3, 1863
> Paint Creek

Dear Daniel and Harrison,

I trust that as you boys receive this letter you are both safe in the Lord's care. Brother John tells us that you two are in Mississippi and near the Vicksburg battle, we here do hope and pray that the conflict there will soon end, as we read it may.

If you haven't heard, Lomira has given birth to a fine, healthy son which she and Schuyler have named Perry. I'm sure this news is the best medicine that Schuyler could possibly hear.

Also, I recently met your parents and sisters and I was quite pleased to see them all in good health and spirits. I was especially impressed by your father who kept saying, "if I was only a younger man I'd be a fighting with my boys." I certainly do believe he would.

We here are all proud of you boys who are putting your lives in danger to preserve our country's freedom and freedom for the enslaved.

> In Faith,
>
> Pastor Neal Hoover
> First Congregational Assembly

I Hear the Bugle's Call

And Harrison received a letter from Katie Welch which, like the others, he never has the notion to share its contents with his tentmates.

> Monday, July 6, 1863
> Cone

Dear Harrison,

I was very pleased to receive your letter of the 26th ult. As I read your descriptions of the places you march through I find it easy to close my eyes and picture the scenes in my mind. You have mentioned in the past your interest in drawing, and I think you should pursue that when you return home.

Back here in Cone the July heat has arrived in full force. My father says that the heat did help turn the wheat as he's busy now with reaping. As the school year ended, I did get permission from the district board to seek summer employment. I was hired part time by Mrs. Heath to clerk in her dry goods store over in East Milan. What money I earn will go to purchasing school supplies for next fall's session. I was approved by the board for next year and with a five dollar a month raise!

We got word of the great Union victories in Pennsylvania and Mississippi. I pray you and Daniel are safe as I know you must have been close to the fighting. On the Fourth we had a celebration behind the schoolhouse. I would guess nearly a hundred turned out for speeches, games and of course, a few fireworks.

I want you and the others to know we all are mighty proud of your service and we pay no mind to those Copperheads who know how to talk but seem to lack a backbone to fight.

I will close this letter now as I thank you for your contribution to our "exchange." I have placed your package in a very becoming brooch and I wear it with pride. Please stay safe.

> Sincerely,
> Katie

We Are All the Same

About this same time Schuyler had some important news for brother John.

Monday, July 20, 1863

Dear John,

I take this pen in a feeble hand to send you some important news. I've been told by the doctors at this hospital that I'm gonna get a discharge in a couple of days. I'm writing this news to you so to keep this a secret from Lomira. By writing this letter now I'm hoping it gets to you before I get home.

My leg wound aint healing enough to allow me to go back to the regiment or even to be sent to the Invalid Corps for camp duty. I am pleased to go home for sure but I do feel like I'm leaving my work only part done. Our brothers are still fighting and doing their part, and I should by all rights be with them. I know with the new one at home Lomira has her hands busy even with all the help you folks have given her. I do appreciate all you and Emma and everyone have done for us. My plan is when I'm discharged I'll take the train up to Toledo. Then a steamer to Detroit. When I get to Ypsilanti I'll find a ride down to our farm and just surprise everyone.

I reckon when that happens you'll hear the commotion from my place to yours. I hope to get home in a week. I would be beholding to you if you'd keep this news quiet from Lomira, Ma and Pa and everyone else till I get there. Until we meet.

Brother Schuyler

As August came about we began wearing out our shoe leather as we marched to Covington, Kentucky and then a bit southeast to Crab Orchard where we have been encamped awaiting further orders.

I Hear the Bugle's Call

Our mail found us and Harrison and I were right happy to get a letter from Schuyler, now promoted to his previous rank, that of Farmer McFall.

Paint Creek
August 3, 1863

Dear Brothers,

I'm writing this letter from the comfort of home and family. Its hard yet for me to take in that I'm actually home. The Army doctors said my leg wound was severe enough not to allow me to get back to Company E or be assigned to the Invalid Corps.

I was released from Camp Dennison a few weeks ago. I wrote John ahead so he would know but I surprised Lomira and the children. I obtained a ride from Ypsilanti and when I got to my farm I just started walking up the path to the house. Lomira was bringing in the eggs about then and when she saw me, the eggs went a flying. To say the least I surprised her. The children then came from the house. They weren't sure who I was at first off. It was a first rate homecoming. Later we and John and Emma rode over and surprised Ma and Pa and our sisters. Of course Ma was a little weepy and I even saw a tear on Pa's cheek.

The doctors say that I'm gonna keep this limp I got, but at least I got my leg. I saw too many boys in the hospitals missing one or both of theirs.

I have kept up as well as I can with the doings of the regiment. John has filled me in on what he hears from you boys too. I came home with troubled feelings of me not being with you boys to finish the job we signed up for last year. I am beholdin to John and Emma and to Thomas and Samantha for taking care of Lomira and the children. Daniel, I've been to your farm and its in fine shape. The crops look healthy and the livestock look fit. I plan to help Thomas and John as much as my leg allows as I know they put in long days trying to keep up.

We Are All the Same

My strength is tolerable for writing so I'll send off a letter to you boys when I can and I hope to hear the latest camp news from you boys when you get the time. Until I hear from you.

Schuyler

And a week or so later Harrison was right pleased a he received a letter which he did admit was from a Miss Welch, though its contents were kept a mystery from me and the others.

Cone
Monday, August 10, 1863

Dear Harrison,

I was most pleased to receive your recent letter. Your description of Vicksburg and the South was fascinating. Your depiction of the plight of the runaway slaves brought tears to my eyes. We here in the North are so far away from those scenes of terror as well as acts of courage by the negroes. We too often at home go about our duties turning a shoulder to the struggles of other human beings. In God's eyes we are all the same. We all here support the heroic acts you and the other men are doing.

From my last class, two graduates have joined with their older brothers. Jason Rice and Billy Hammond signed up in Monroe as drummers. It was said they practiced a good bit so they would be accepted. I do worry for them as I see them as school boys not soldiers.

My work clerking with Mrs. Heath has gone well. I've been able to save a bit of money for school. I have learned that a dry goods store is quite the place to learn the news of the day, or as some would describe it as gossip. The weather here is the typical hot, dry days of August.

I Hear the Bugle's Call

We've heard your brother Schuyler has come home which we are all grateful for. But I do wish you and Daniel were on your way home soon also. With the victories the North has won, the rebels must be near their end. It would seem the Christian thing for them to end the mutual suffering and stop this war.

I wanted to also let you know I've gotten quite the number of adoring comments concerning the brooch I wear constantly. I've received many questions about the brooch holds inside but I refuse to answer. And like you said in your last letter, when you return home we will happily respond.

I must end now so say hello to your brothers and stay safe.

Sincerely,
Katie

And we both received a fine letter from Brother John.

Paint Creek
Friday, August 14, 1963

Dear Daniel and Harrison,

I truly hope that this letter finds you both safe and healthy. As I'm sure you know Schuyler has returned home safely. He appears in general to be in good health, the leg wound does affect his walking and getting around. He says it don't bother him none but I can tell that aint the whole truth. Schuyler's homecoming has certainly been a Godsend for Lomira. With the birth of their new babe and Schuyler being home, she says that their lives can now pick up from where they were interrupted last year. Pa and Ma are also glad to see Schuyler return home. Their only wish now is for you boys to join your brother and come home.

Some other news that might catch your interest concerns the local farm prices. I was able to sell nearly 394 pounds of wool from your sheep and mine for 62 cents a pound. With selling a few lambs at 12 dollars per head we gained about $400.00. Our wheat came in at 25 bushels for the acre and our clover fields provided enough to surely get through the coming winter.

Thomas and I went together and bought a stump machine from Ernest Moore. We figure we can hire it out when we don't need it.

The draft has begun in the county. Most men I've talked to figure to volunteer before the government drags them in. Being here safe while you boys volunteered does trouble me at times. I know we all agreed I'd stay back to manage things, but I still feel I'm not doing my rightful share.

The local papers are calling the Ninth Corps the "flying corps" for all the traveling you've been up to.

I'll be ending now so take care and as Pa says, "keep your heads down."

Brother John

Now as we know Schuyler was sent home. We knew he'd be wanting to know what the news of his old regiment. Harrison and I proceeded to inform him of our march to Vicksburg and the sights we saw of the town and the Rebels.

Monday, August 17, 1863
Covington, Kentucky

Dear Schuyler,

We have received your letter of early August and Harrison and I are much relieved knowing you are now back home. We can certainly imagine the happiness Lomira and your little ones must now feel with your presence.

We can certainly understand your wanting to return to the regiment, and we all would have welcomed you back as brother and fellow soldier. You certainly have shown courage under fire and devotion to duty. The Army has decided wisely in sending you home now to wage "battle" on the corn weevils and other attacking enemies.

As you may know, the regiment was near Vicksburg at the time of surrender. In fact Sergeant Maltman, James Masters, John Yaw, Harrison and I actually saw the surrender papers being exchanged. It was quite a sight as a staff officer from General Pemberton exchanged the surrender terms with an officer from Grant's staff. We found out later that the terms were unconditional surrender with parole for all.

We then had a chance to walk around the town for a short spell. It was a sight I'd never seen before. The rebel soldiers and townspeople had burrowed themselves in the ground like prairie dogs to keep safe from our artillery. We were told that food was near run out. In the last four days people were left to butcher the dogs and mules and even rats. It didn't have to happen. As sad as we are for their plight, the rebel command could have put an end to this suffering weeks ago.

We've been busy since Vicksburg. The 17th went on to Jackson, Mississippi and for about a week last month we laid siege to that town. They finally surrendered and we were then put to tearing up the railroad in those parts. We did enjoy ripping up the tracks and putting the rails to fire. We also got to forage which proved very successful. You'd be proud of your old company when it comes to scaring up our own rations. We found plenty of pork, sweet yams, and molasses for our stomachs. As I write this we are back up north near Covington, Kentucky.

We hoped that the fall of Vicksburg would end the war in the West, but these stubborn rebels don't think they're licked yet.

Also, you may be interested to know that Delos Phillips has been promoted to Lieutenant of Co E. Also, I know you'd really be surprised to know I was promoted to corporal a few months back. Being corporal comes with more duties assigned then I care for but I manage.

Harrison and the other boys from home send their respects and wish you and everyone well. Write us when you can. Keep me up on my farm.

                          Daniel and Harrison

                          Company E
                          1st Brigade
                          1st Division
                          9th Corps
                          Army of the Tennessee

Our regiment remained near Crab Orchard until September 10th.

Prior to breaking camp we passed a few weeks of routine camp life. When not in battle, boredom is our enemy. Some of the men surrender to the vice of gambling be it with cards or dice which they call "chuck-a-luck." Harrison and I have no desire to join in but as we observe, this game seems to be about betting on the odds of a dice throw. Too many losers and too few winners seem to be the outcome.

One camp activity which we heartily join is a game of baseball. The game played here is much like we know back home. Our company takes on all challengers and I might add Harrison and I are rather powerful strikers. The game is a first rate way to pass a few hours before its back to the work at hand.

On September 9th we received orders to prepare to leave for Knoxville, Tennessee the next morning with eight days rations in our knapsacks and four more days carried in the wagons.

We are told the distance from Crab Orchard to Knoxville is about 150 miles.

Although we have been in this army and on many a march it is still a rough chore to carry 40 rounds of cartridges, a knapsack filled with a change of clothes, 1/2 tent, oil cloth, blanket, and eight days of food.

We marched about ten miles and camped near Mt. Vernon. Reveille was

I Hear the Bugle's Call

around 3 a.m. and we marched until sun up. The sun was shining brightly that day and the heat was unmerciful. I dare say a whole lot of men dropped out of the march and Harrison and I were close to joining the troops who surrendered to the heat. We heard a young soldier from Company I died from the devilish heat.

We marched about 15 miles that day and though Harrison, James Masters, Sergeant Maltman and I didn't drop out, we did slow our pace a good deal and didn't come into camp till after sundown. We were so tired that we just dropped on the nearest patch of grass and commenced to sleep.

Next morning we got on the march before daylight and after about eight miles camped near London, Kentucky which was about fifty miles from the Cumberland Gap.

We marched over 150 miles in the last two weeks along winding mountain roads. Our regiment came across some 2,500 rebel prisoners taken recently. The rebel commander, General Frazer was in splendid appearance, but his men were dirty and appeared as ignorant as mules. They were being taken north to Camp Chase in Ohio. Along the way the mail caught up with us and the pay officer did as well. Harrison and I were doubly paid as we both got mail and our pay. Though our pay did have deductions for our uniforms which brought my pay down some, Harrison received his now frequent letter from Cone and I received a fine letter from Ma and Pa.

We Are All the Same

Cone, Michigan
Wednesday, September 9, 1863

Dear Harrison,

I happily received your letter of August 15th and am amazed at the traveling your regiment has been doing. You, Daniel, and the other men must be foot sore from the miles you've marched across the South.

In the papers they've been called your corps "Burnside's Geography class" for all the territory seen. I do hope this letter finds you and Daniel safe and rested.

The new school year has begun and I've got twenty eight students enrolled. Of course with harvest season upon us I've yet to see the older students which is about twelve of my enrollment. I do enjoy the first few days of school as the wee ones come for the first time. I have four young ones that have come with their older siblings. Needless to say they have a bit a fear in their faces, but that fades soon off.

I've heard that two of my graduates from last year may be near you as they were assigned to the 20th Michigan as musicians. Everyone here prays for their safety and for all bravely serving our country.

I'm through clerking for Mrs. Heath, but I may go back to her store next summer. I enjoyed the work, but even more I had many pleasant conversations with the customers.

My Pa has heard from your parents that Schuyler is doing well at home and I'm sure his wife and children are most happy to have him with them. I do wish this dreadful war would end soon so you too could return to your family and others that care.

I will end now as I must prepare the studies for tomorrow. Please write when you can.

Sincerely,
Katie

I Hear the Bugle's Call

Cone, Michigan
Monday, September 14, 1863

Dear Daniel and Harrison,

I thought you boys would be surprised to get a letter from your parents. I know we don't write much but your Pa and I aint use to letter writing.

We keep up with you boys from talking with John and now with Schuyler. It is a good feeling to have Schuyler home. He's got a limp, but he seems to be able to do a good days job around the farm. I know Lomira is sure glad to have him home. We do pray that you boys will also be a coming home with an end to this devilish war. It makes my heart ache so every time I hear of one of our boys from Cone or Augusta aint coming home to their families.

Harrison, I know you'd like to hear that we see that sweet Katie Welch at sermon every Sabbath. She says she writes often to you. Now you make sure to write her when you can. You have to admire a young lady like her that has a good head on her shoulders and is a fine Christian.

Pa sends his best as always. With fall being so busy for him I worry that he does too much. He just ignores my warnings about overdoing at his age. We all know he's been a hard worker all his life and we aint going to change that.

I'll be ending this but I'll enclose this letter in a box of homemade baking I've done today.

Boys, we pray daily for your safety.

Your loving parents,
Pa, Ma

We arrived at the Cumberland Gap on Sunday the 20th. The Gap is an open valley between some mountains, which provided us some first rate sights as we marched along.

From the Gap we marched to Morristown which was almost 50 miles hence.

At Morristown we finally got to ride some rail cars rather than wearing out more shoe leather. East Tennessee is a most beautiful country with fast moving streams and plentiful forests.

The train took us to Knoxville and we shared the train with General Burnside who would make Knoxville his headquarters.

The General's appearance is quite simple. His coat has no shoulder straps and on his head is a round, tall hat. As we have had him as our commander for most of the last year, we know him to be a quiet, simple man, not a "parade dandy." We've been told many in East Tennessee look to him and our Corps as liberators from the marauding plague brought on by the rebels.

As the month of September neared its end Harrison and I had time to work on a couple of letters. First to our brother John and his wife.

Friday, September 25, 1863
Knoxville, Tennessee

Dear John and Emma,

Harrison and I have been too busy marching lately to keep up on our letter writing. But finally our regiment has settled down here in Knoxville, Tennessee. Being on the move so much our mail has a devil of a time finding us. We did get your letter of the 14th ult. and we are much obliged for the farm news. I'm especially indebted to you and Thomas for keeping up my farm since I left.

We're also might happy to see that Schuyler got home and though he may be afflicted some, he can still pull his own weight when it comes to his chores. Me and Harrison plan on writing him so he can keep up with his old company.

As I said we've been on the march pretty near every day for the last two months. After the fall of Vicksburg our regiment took part in the siege of Jackson, Mississippi – its capital. The rebs gave up after about a week then

I Hear the Bugle's Call

we was put to work tearing up the railroads so the rebs couldn't come back and use them. In August we marched back up to Kentucky and spent most of the month skirmishing with General Bragg's men around Covington and Crab Orchard, Kentucky. Finally around the 10th of this month we're sent to Knoxville. We've heard rumors that Confederate General Longstreet has come west from Virginia with a few divisions and joined Bragg. With that a possibility we expect some real excitement to commence soon.

We don't hear much from the East. The last we heard General Meade and the Army of the Potomac was successful in Pennsylvania, but that was in July. What's been going on lately we don't know.

Harrison and I are in good health and though fall is about to start, the weather here is still tolerable. It's hard to fancy at times that we've been gone for a bit over a year. As Harrison and I think back to mustering in, it seems like we've been in the Army for ten years at least. We surely hope this fall will be our last away from home. I must end for I hear the bugle's call. I hope its for mail.

> Brothers Daniel and Harrison,
>
> Company E
> 3rd Brigade
> 1st Division
> 9th Corps
> Army of the Tennessee

And also a letter to brother Schuyler.

> Saturday, September 26, 1863
> Knoxville, Tennessee

Dear Schuyler,

Me and Harrison trust this letter finds you, Lomira and the young ones first rate. We can surely imagine how busy you, John, and Thomas must be at this time of year. We would sure like to be there to help with the harvesting. When you can let us know how the crops did.

As I write this, the 17th Regiment has gotten to Knoxville, Tennessee. In the past month we've been busy knocking heads with Bragg's men. Rumor has it that Longstreet is on his way to help Bragg so General Burnside decided we needed to get to Tennessee to face what may come.

Company E continues to pull our regular duties of picket or of foraging. On my last picket duty I "drawed some apples, peaches, and even some molasses." Harrison, James, and Andrew Lilly thought I done right smart.

We've been getting a few drafted men lately. It aint easy welcoming these men as comrades when we know they were forced to put on the uniform. Colonel Luce has told everyone to put aside any ill feelings as we all are the same. However they got here, they are part of the 17th Michigan. We shall see when they hear the rebel yell for the first time which way their feet carry them.

Recently we learned that Delos Phillips has a brother Darius, and lo and behold he has a sutler's wagon near our regiment. We aint sure it that's just a strange turn of events or something more.

I'll have to end this now as its about time for company drill and inspection.

Give everyone our kind regards.

                    Daniel and Harrison,

                    Company E
                    3rd Brigade
                    1st Division
                    9th Corps
                    Army of the Tennessee

Fall was seen in east Tennessee each morning as September was nearing its end. Though we looked forward to more temperate weather, we know that here in the highlands cold and snow weren't far away.

Harrison and I talked one evening about our first year in the Army and what we've been through. Though Schuyler is safe at home he is certainly missed. We've lost too many good men from our company since August last. We've marched from Maryland to Mississippi. We've seen the elephant and we've seen the backs of the enemy a fair amount.

I mentioned to Harrison that we should be proud of how we have taken to soldier life and looked out for each other.

We continue to hear peace rumors, but we know they aint worth much. This war aint ending without more fighting and we both predicted that we will see our share before this year is out.

Harrison ended our conversation with a prediction, "Brother, with your soldier skills and my luck, we'll be home this time next year telling everyone our stories, and some may even be true." I nodded with a smile and responded, "Brother, I agree and I promise not to decipher which is which."

We had no way of knowing the coming of fall would cause one of our predictions coming true with an unexpected result.

We Are All the Same

I Hear the Bugle's Call

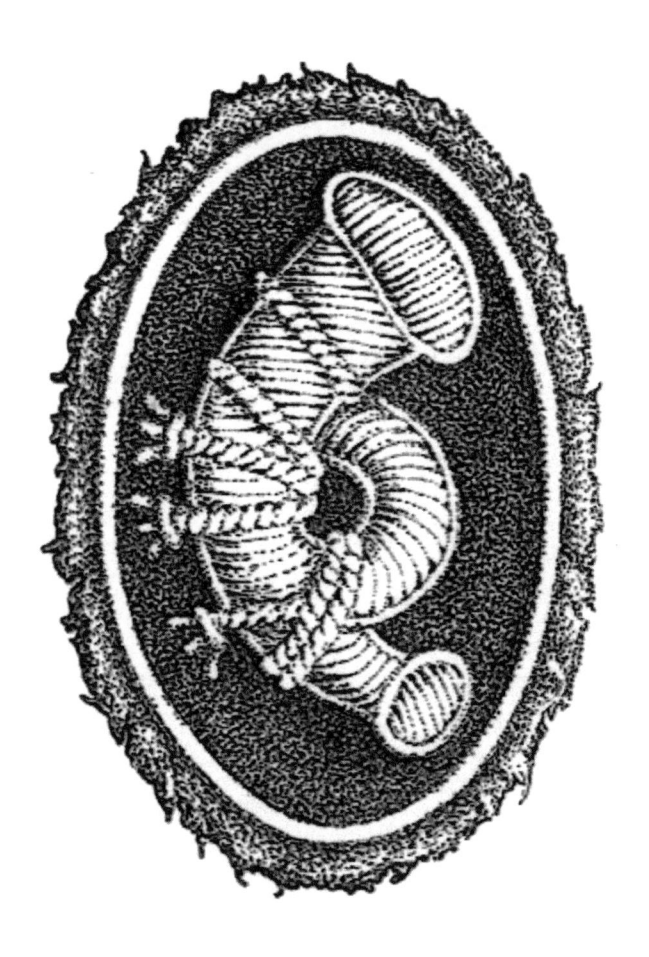

An Angry Wind
October 1863 – April 1864

October found our regiment marching around eastern Tennessee. As the month began we were camped near Knoxville. We expected a fight between here and a place called Bristol.

We and the rest of the Third Brigade were ordered to the depot. The regiment had to wait for space, but we were finally put on the cars the next morning. We heard that there were 8,000 rebels trapped and ready for capture. The rebels seem to feel they have to hold on to this area at all costs. Should that be true, I don't look kindly to the days to come.

We rode until reaching a place called Blue Springs at sundown. A fight had started earlier that day and was still going on.
We started towards the firing as the rebels had been driven back a few miles. We went about a mile and halted for the night. We passed among the dead and met some of our wounded. It seemed to Harrison and me that Sunday morning would bring a violent sunrise.

We fell in line of battle about 5 a.m. after drawing sixty rounds of cartridges.

About 7 a.m. our division commander, General Ferrero, rode along our line giving words of encouragement. Our division was posted in the center and as we moved forward we first had to march through an open field of at least 100 rods. Much to our surprise we found that the rebels had turned tail during the night. Sergeant Maltman commented to Harrison and me that, "this here Sunday is a better day for a church social than a battle anyway." We happily nodded in agreement.

We spent that Sunday following the rebels for near twenty miles without finding any of them. On Tuesday, we started back to Blue Springs expecting a ride, but instead had to march. Some of the officers had sent their horses back on the cars so they also had to take it on foot. It did raise the spirits of us privates and corporals to see them "enjoying" the rocky and hilly roads on the double quick as we all marched to camp.

We took the cars from Morristown to Knoxville, arriving there around noon on Friday. Knoxville greeted us with three days of rain.

We hear that Michigan's draft quota is about 7,000 men as President Lincoln calls for 600,000 more. All of us do pray that this is the last call for men and spring brings us peace.

As October was ending we found ourselves outside of Knoxville and to our great relief we have orders to prepare winter quarters.

We have a rather doubtful supply line over the mountains and the surroundings don't look good for foraging as the citizens and their farms are in poor shape.

As we start to settle in, some from our regiment have been chosen to go home and recruit. Company E seems to always be left out of such duty. Harrison and I would not mind going home to shake the bushes for recruits.

Recently, we had some officer changes as Lieutenant Phillips has been promoted to captain and command of our company and Billings and Harmon became first and second lieutenants.

Captain Campbell has resigned. "Why" has been a real topic around the camp, some tell of a problem with government funds, but we may never know for sure. Harrison and both agree that we will miss him. He was with us since Ypsilanti and led us well in battle—so goes war.

We received some mail at long last and enjoyed a letter from brother Schuyler.

An Angry Wind

Paint Creek
Saturday, October 10, 1863

Dear Daniel and Harrison,

I received your letter of the 26th ult. and thought I would take this opportunity to write back to my younger brothers. As you may tell my chicken scratches with pen are getting a bit stronger. As time goes by I'm getting my strength up to almost like it was, but I do use my cane more than I care to. I brought home a fine looking cane, that was made for me by a woodcarver back in the Frederick hospital. I put that one away and use a strong hickory rod I found here on the farm. No use getting the good one broke or splintered.

I appreciate the news from the company that you boys pass along to me. I do miss not being with all of you even though I know those cold fall winds must be biting on picket. Send my regards to Sergeant Maltman, John Mason, and James Masters. When I got home I made it a promise to myself to stop by their families when I could to pay my respects.

We been reading about the drafted men going in now and quite a few men from our county are rushing to sign up before they get their names picked. Their patriotic spirit is appreciated, but where were they before large bonuses were offered by the towns and states? What we signed up for aint near what goes for a bonus today.

We've been reading in the papers about the Ninth Corps marching around Tennessee. I would guess that you boys are near to setting in for winter quarters soon. This devilish war drags on when just a battle or two more could end it. But that's my ramblings.

Daniel, your farm looks to be in good shape. John, Thomas, and I brought in a good yield of corn from the far east 15 acres and the livestock should make it through the winter in good shape. We did have to mend your roof on the house as a huge storm came this way last week. Its mended fine and it'll take a strong winter. That storm took down two barns over on the Talladay property—no injuries thank God.

I Hear the Bugle's Call

Lomira and the young ones are doing fine and so are Ma and Pa. The change in the weather has given them both the twinges but no different from other years.

The church women are preparing a package for you boys so be looking out for mail call soon.

Take care and keep your heads down.

Brother Schuyler

It was good to hear news from home and Harrison and I shared it with the Augusta men.

Also arriving in the mail was a letter for Harrison, which also came with a box of baked goods, stamps, envelopes, and jams. Harrison allowed to share in this bounty, but he chose not to share the letter.

Cone
Monday, October 12, 1863

Dear Harrison,

I received your letter of the 25th ult. and enjoyed your description of the birds and animals your Company has come across.

I have shared your information with my class as some of them also have family or friends in Tennessee.

As I have mentioned, my class should have about twenty-five students but with harvesting still not done I have yet to see a full class. With a full class comes the usual bouts with coughs and fevers.

My parents heard from your parents that Schuyler is doing well back home on his farm. How we all wish you and your brother were also home with us. My mother caught me glancing at my brooch in the mirror and asked me why

I wear it so often. I just responded, "It's just such a pretty thing." She has no idea what it contains. I hope you have kept my contribution somewhere safe.

The ladies of the Cone Church are putting together some sewed items and baked goods for our boys in uniform. I plan on making sure one of these special boxes is sent your way. I'll include enough "Treasures" for you and Daniel.

I must end now as I am to prepare my lessons for tomorrow.

Please be safe,
Katie

As we had the time, I wrote for both of us a letter to the family.

Lenoir, Tennessee
Thursday, October 22, 1863

Dear Ma and Pa and Sisters,

Harrison and I got your letter of September and enjoyed reading about home. Since our last letter we have been very busy marching around the state of Tennessee.

Earlier this month our division moved from Knoxville to Blue Springs then marched back to Knoxville. On the 20th we marched to a place called Louden and now we're at a town called Lenoir, not far from Loudon. We've been marching to and fro cause of goings on by the rebels under General Longstreet. The rebel cavalry seem to pop up like moles from the ground, then disappear.

The Ninth Corps has the Michigan Regiments—2nd, 8th, 20th and 17th. Together with the rest of the corps we've traveled pretty near 2,100 miles in a year. Most of the miles have been on foot so you can bet most of us are in

need of some new brogans. Mine and Harrison's are tolerable for now.
Fall is arriving with cold nights and some frost in the mornings.
We hear rumors that we may stay here for the winter. Harrison and I have been foraging for some usable wood and logs in case we do stay put. With one winter under our belt we aint new recruits when it comes to building a shelter.

We hope everyone is healthy and doing well. How was the fall harvest?

We guess, Ma, that you've been busy with the girls on your preserving. We'd be right pleased if you could send us some of your preserves. And surely, some cornbread would go mighty fine with the sorghum.

Harrison and I are in good health. With fall comes the coughs and fevers but we have been lucky so far. One of the problems of us moving so much, mail is slow to catch up. We hope if we do stay here the mail will find us quicker. If you could send us some newspapers, we'd share the news with the others. I and Harrison will end now as we have company inspection and as Corporal, I got to help roust up the men.

          Your sons,

          Daniel and Harrison
          Company E
          3rd Brigade
          1st Division
          9th Corps
          Army of the Tennessee

By early November we had our cabin built as Harrison, Maltman, Mason, Masters, and I worked together on what sure looked like a tolerable structure with boards, tree boughs, and mud blocking the wind, and a dry straw floor. On Friday, November 6th, late, the Third Brigade was ordered to prepare to move. None of us were inclined to leave, but when the bugles sound, we move. We rode the cars to Knoxville and camped, waiting our orders.

The reason for our deployment was a cavalry raid at Morristown. The rebels attacked the Seventh Ohio and Second Tennessee, then withdrew. That being the case, we didn't pursue, but returned to camp.

As we return to our camp we hope to settle in for the winter. Last year we had the Rapahannock River betwixt us and rebels, this year it's the Tennessee. While on picket we still have a chat or trade with the rebels as we endure the weather together.

As November pressed on, fall was certainly in appearance as the trees were in brilliant colors and flocks of birds were seen winging south.

Mid November came on the wings of a cold and angry wind that brought rain and, as we would soon discover, the return of the "elephant."

On the morning of November 14th the order came down to pack all baggage and be ready to move. At around noon the bugles called assembly and our regiment followed the Second Michigan. Not long after sundown we halted in some woods in battle lines facing the rebels.

Early the next morning we marched back to Lenoir Station, arriving about noon. We had just a while to brew coffee and draw out some hardtack, then, at midday, we took position with the brigade behind the station.

While we were resting in position we witnessed other troops passing to the rear. The wind was bitter but orders were given for only one fire for each company as the rebels were nearby.

Early on the morning of the 16th we were told by Captain Phillips that our regiment was ordered to form the rear guard as 100 or more baggage wagons were being emptied. Food, clothes, and blankets were there for the taking as the wagons were being torched and the horses assigned for artillery duty. I went with Harrison and Sergeant Maltman as we quickly grabbed what food we could, such as dried meat and flour, and as many blankets as we could carry. Our thought was, better in our knapsacks than in the rebels' hands. By sunup it was apparent to all that a retreat was about to begin.

Captain Phillips told us that the Second Division of our corps would hold the hills around a place called Campbell's Station.

I Hear the Bugle's Call

Sometime after 7 a.m. our brigade led by Colonel Humphrey filed on to the road. Our regiment was the last behind the Twentieth Michigan and the Second Michigan.

Companies E, K, and some from Company G were sent out as skirmishers. Companies E and the rest of Company G were the reserve as Company K deployed along both sides of the road. Our regiment was to keep within a few hundred rods of the brigade.

We had walked about a mile from Lenoir when we heard gunfire behind us as a Union cavalry detachment rode by. They said that they had finished torching the abandoned wagons as Confederate skirmishers appeared.

We passed by some stragglers, including an old looking private, who appeared to be a cook, as he was sitting with pots and kettles draped about his shoulders. Harrison and I noticed he was smoking his pipe while he watched calmly as if he was sitting on his front porch back home. After a few rebel shots kicked up dirt near him, he stood up quickly and away he skedaddled with his wares making a deafening racket.

We traveled for three or four miles along a railroad track. Then we headed northeast along a muddy road through hills and woods. This type of march causes fatigue quickly, plus the sun was adding its heat. I mentioned to Harrison, "These knapsacks are starting to weigh heavy on my back." He responded, "we could sure use those baggage trains about now."

As we were passing over a hill I could see a rebel line coming our way. I said to Harrison and James Masters, "Boys, look sharp to our right. I don't like that vision no way." James Masters responded, "Daniel, we only wish that it were a vision. We are about to earn our money today," As far as the eye could see, was a double line of gray and butternut. We were slowed as we had to scramble amidst fallen trees. The rebels skirmishers were within rifle range. And troops forming a battleline behind them were spied by all of us.

We continued through a confusion of thick brush, fallen timber, and steep hills. We finally got to the edge of an open field when we heard a shout, "Halt, come here!" I turned to see the rebels behind us as I heard a bullet buzz nearby. The rebel officer seemed to wave us to come back, but none of us were inclined to obey that order.

We all started to run, and in my desire to live another day, I became separated from Harrison. Sergeant Maltman and I began running and dodging behind trees as musket balls kicked up dirt and found tree bark. We both threw off our knapsacks and I found that I was ahead of him as I had some advantage in size.

I reached the regiment as they had formed on the west side of the ford across Turkey Creek. The Confederates had crossed above and below the ford. At this point I looked to see who was still with me. I was surprised to finally realize Harrison was not in sight, nor was Sergeant Maltman. I wanted to search for them, but the rebels began pouring fire on us and Colonel Comstock ordered us to, "hold the creek!"

The rebels were all around us, pelting everything with musket balls as thick as bees around a hive. I saw at least one of our colorbearers go down as Captain Tyler of Company G called out, "Remember South Mountain!"

Major Swift then took the colors from the hand of the next brave bearer to fall and shouted, "Men form on me!" I quickly moved over closer to his position while firing as fast as I could.

Corporal Curtis took possession of the flag and Major Swift called for firing at-will as the rebels came near the creek. Our brigade was about ¾ to a mile away.

Our rally stunned the enemy for a time, which led Major Swift to call for a countercharge. I and what was left of our regiment rose and, with a yell, startled the rebels so completely that they turned and quickly retreated.

Knowing that we didn't have the force to continue the attack, Major Swift called for a halt to rejoin the brigade and march to Campbell's Station.

Union artillery became more active against the Confederate advance which allowed what was left of our three companies time to make our way to the brigade line of battle.

Our regiment formed on the left of the brigade and we continued our march toward Campbell's Station. Soon the whole Confederate force continued to press their attack and the brigade halted near a rail fence. This short volley slowed the rebels which allowed the brigade to fall back to a road that was held by our main force.

During the afternoon Company E, or what was left of it, was sent out as skirmishers, but the fighting was without spirit on both sides. At dusk we began to fall back to Knoxville. As we marched I asked everyone I saw if they had seen Harrison. I was desperate for news of any kind. Captain Phillips said he'd start checking with other commanders for any information on all our casualties.

We trudged into Knoxville before dawn on the 17th. Our division was assigned a line along a river called the Holston, north to a place called Fort Sanders. As more of Company E reunited, we soon noticed Sergeant Maltman was still missing. John Yaw thought he saw Maltman go down early as we were retreating. I mentioned that I had seen Maltman last as we were being chased by rebels and bullets. We hoped to see him alive and soon.

The regiment began digging in as a defense line would soon be needed. Longstreet's men weren't expected to give us any break. Captain Phillips came around to talk to our company and fill us in on the bad news of the last few days. He told us that, of the confirmed casualties, George Hathaway from Chelsea was killed, also Walter Maxfield from Jackson County. George McMichael from Saline was wounded, also Sergeant Maltman was found with a head wound. Possibly captured was James Morgan and also Harrison. The Captain added that Harrison may also have been wounded, based on an unofficial report.

I now had the duty of writing home the terrible news. My thought was to write to Schuyler knowing he'd best understand and he could pass on the news to the rest of the family. I waited a few days before writing, hoping I'd get some good news as Harrison would make his way back to our company. But, I decided, as a few more days passed it was time to write a short note to Schuyler with, perhaps, a more detailed letter to follow.

An Angry Wind

Thursday, November 26, 1863
Knoxville, Tennessee

Dear Brother,

I have some sad news to pass along to you and our family. Our brother Harrison is missing and perhaps captured by the rebels as of the 16th. I aint had the time to write sooner as our regiment has been fighting the rebels as a rear guard for near the past two weeks.

Right now as I write this we are at Knoxville under siege by General Longstreet's divisions. I aint sure if and when mail will get out of the city. As the rebels came on, Harrison and I became separated as we fell back with two other companies of the 17th. John Yaw heard that Harrison and another soldier were seen going into a shed or barn as the rebels neared. I heard tell that he might have been wounded but that aint for sure. I must admit I had felt responsible for the boy's safety. I don't feel I did all I could to keep him out of trouble. I know you would understand the situation better. I'm asking you to tell our folks, John, and the others up front so they don't get the news from others. Also, let them know that men missing do return safe—it don't mean the worse. But, I'd not let on that Harrison might be wounded.

I'm safe here for now and I'll write more when the commotion quiets down.

Daniel,

Company E
3rd Brigade
1st Division
9th Corps
Army of the Tennessee

The last week of November was a time of off and on skirmishing. We were given the sad news that on the 25th Lieutenant Colonel Comstock was killed by sharpshooters. We were all dug in our rifle pits, which afforded only a slight bit of safety. When we had to venture out to draw rations, get wood, or any other need we would draw fire like crows in a cornfield.

With the loss of Harrison my tentmates included John Mason and James Masters. We heard Sergeant Maltman survived his wound and is back at the field hospital. That was some welcome good news for a change.

The rebels plan on starving us out of Knoxville so we've been put on short rations. We can only draw 1/2 meat, 1/4 bread and no coffee. And when I say bread I mean what looks like a brick size chunk of tree bark. We have all become good traders as every soldier looks for an edible deal. As the siege wears on, the men I talk with feel that Grant will soon send aid as it would be a foolish waste of lives to try and fight our way out. It is a given that we are outnumbered by a least a division.

About the morning of November 29th the Confederates sent one division against the area called Fort Sanders. This is highland a little northwest of Knoxville. But we had planned for such a visit as the area was well guarded, with telegraph wire stretched between tree stumps, a ditch of a width of four to six feet and depth of twelve feet, and well placed artillery batteries.

The rebel attack failed with hundreds of Confederate losses and a handful of Union.

Following the Fort Sanders ruckus both sides carried out our often practiced routine of quickly arranged truces. Both sides would consent to a cease fire for wood gathering and bartering. We all knew this was frowned upon by higher command, but there are times when us lowly corporals and privates decide what's best for us.

At noon on December 1st a statement from General Burnside was read informing us about General Grant's success in defeating General Bragg's army. This good news could only mean our distress would soon end. I finally found the time and the relative safety to write a letter to Brother John informing him in more detail about Harrison being missing and the action of the last month.

An Angry Wind

Tuesday, December 1, 1863
Knoxville, Tennessee

Dear John and family,

I trust my letter of the 26th ult. has reached you with the sad news of Harrison. Since I wrote, he continues to be missing and I fear captured. If he is captured, there is a chance he could be exchanged as we have a herd of sesesh prisoners of our own.

To the best of my thinking, Harrison and I were separated on our march to Knoxville as our company was assigned at the rear of our forces.

As I write this letter, our regiment is at Knoxville under siege. Two days ago we were involved with the rebels at a place called Fort Sanders outside our lines. Our flag saw victory but at a cost of about 100 union men and maybe 700 to 800 rebels. General Longstreet sent three brigades at a hilltop that we had reinforced with telegraph wire and was also protected by a deep ditch. We captured hundreds of arms and three stands of color.

Three companies of the 17th had the task of holding off the rebels from our division rear.

Campbell's Station lay at a crossroads on the way to Knoxville. It was a race between our men and Longstreet's to capture that location first. As we arrived first, the rebels were quick on our heels.

The rebels attacked on both of our flanks, but we held them off. While this attack was happening I believe Harrison and a few others were trapped in a tobacco barn or shed. This was when he was taken and is believed held as a prisoner. We have not heard of any prisoner exchange, so I fear Harrison and James Morgan, who was also captured, may be heading for Richmond and prison. Sergeant Maltman had a head wound, which we pray is not serious and Corporal Dewel had a hand wound.

As the siege continues we are down on rations to a small bit of bread made of corn meal and the cob, no coffee, and half pound of meat at best a day. We feel that the rebels cannot break us as we have a strong defense line. Rumors of Grant sending reinforcements and supplies keep up our spirits. Captain Phillips is our company commander as Captain Campbell resigned back in October. Captain Phillips spoke to some of us while on picket and he mentioned the wind, biting, blowing from the North. He called it "an angry wind." As I look back on the last fortnight, I sadly agree.

Pass the word to all that I am fine and tell everyone to keep a strong heart for Harrison's safe return. The mail moves when it can so I hope you will receive this soon.

Daniel,

Company E
3rd Brigade
1st Division
9th Corps
Army of the Tennessee

I continue to think of Harrison as missing rather than captured. We've seen men return to our regiment daily who we thought captured. They wander back from the field hospital or from having taken up with another unit as we retreated back to Knoxville. What adds to my optimism about Harrison is that Sergeant Maltman has returned after his head wound. As I awake each morning, I scan the encampment for the sight of my young brother striding up to the campfire asking, "what's in the pan today?"

Saturday the 5th of December broke some good news as the rebels have pulled away as their siege ended. I do confess that we were near our limits as supplies and morale were both in scant supply.

On Sunday, General Burnside and General Sherman came by the perimeter looking at the rebel works. Later in the day Captain Swift addressed the regiment congratulating the 17th for its courage in facing the hardships and dangers. An order was also read from General Burnside, General Potter and General Ferrero praising the troops for their conduct during the siege.

All this high talk is fine, but us enlisted men were more concerned about

An Angry Wind

when we get fed right and get clean uniforms.

As the fighting seems to have ended for perhaps a brief attempt at peace, it is a clearly seen fact that the Seventeenth has faced the angry wind of battle. Our regiment lost at least ninety men in three weeks of fighting. But through all of this we came through, showing the enemy that we Michigan men had the spirit to defend what's right and honorable.

As the days of December passed, fighting continued. As the siege ended we took up orders to follow the rebels east. After a heated skirmish, including cavalry, we fell back to Blaines Crossroads twenty miles or so from Knoxville.

It is said that we have about 75,000 men in four corps here. Supplies most come up the Chattanooga River and we are in dire need of winter clothes and boots.

The rumors of camp consist of where we go next. We've heard that General Burnside has gone to Washington and maybe the Ninth Corps will follow. We could also find Tennessee as our winter quarters, only time will tell. The pay wagon finally caught up with us and that was a welcome sight for sure. With the pay also came the mail and a letter arrived for Harrison from Katie Welch. I decided not to open it but keep it for safe keeping. I know if Harrison remained missing for much longer he would be considered captured. Should that be the case I would feel it only proper that a letter from me should be written to her. I don't look forward to such a task and pray it ain't necessary.

I did receive a welcomed letter from Schuyler, which was what I needed to ease my mind some.

I Hear the Bugle's Call

Paint Creek
Tuesday, December 15, 1863

Dear Daniel,

I received your letter of the 26th ult. with much sadness. I certainly was not prepared to hear about the heap of fighting that the regiment has been taking on in Tennessee. I figured that Company E would be sitting in winter quarters not fighting rear guard attacks.

I know what missing in action can mean, but I pray that by the time this letter finds that Harrison has returned to the company. Don't fret that his missing is any of your fault. He can take care of himself as I know he has learned soldiering right well. I'm sure whatever befell him was not something you could head off.

I try to keep Ma and Pa calmed about Harrison, telling them how Harrison being missing don't mean the worst. But between you and me, I know the odds of him showing himself aint strong.

We read that your division is held up in Knoxville by the rebels in some kind of siege. We also hear that Grant has support heading your way and perhaps, as I am writing this, the siege is over.

Don't worry about us here. Except for the usual winter twinges us old folks are doing well.

We will all be praying for your safety and Harrison's safe return.

Lomira and Emma are preparing a Christmas box of clothes and food. Be looking for it and hopefully you and Harrison can both share it.

Brother Schuyler

On Christmas afternoon I had the time off from picket to write a letter home to my parents and sisters.

An Angry Wind

Thursday, December 25, 1863
Blaines Crossroads, Tennessee

Dear Ma, Pa and Sisters,

Well as I write this letter it is Christmas Day. Last Christmas our regiment was back East at Falmouth, Virginia and one year later we are sitting at a small town East of Knoxville, Tennessee.

Harrison is still declared missing, which don't mean the worst. When a soldier is missing that usually means the rebels have him. We have a mess of their men too, so exchanges of men take place. I expect any day now to see him and some other men walking into our camp as happy to see us as we are to see them, so Ma and Pa, don't fret none. Harrison has learned a lot in the army and can take care of himself. He aint the green farmboy of awhile back.

Our camp here has four corps, which we hear is about 75,000 men. That's quite a passel.

General Burnside has been sent east to Washington, which makes us think we may follow. General Parke has taken over for Burnside.

I do say that we are in a sorry shape for clothes and food. The siege at Knoxville, which you may have heard was rather severe. Grant sent forces to cause Longstreet to skedaddle so now we are awaiting supplies to arrive from Chattanooga. The pay master finally caught up with us last week, which was greatly appreciated. You will find enclosed $15.00 to add to my account.

This past month has been a rough spell with not only Harrison missing, but Sergeant Maltman got a head wound and Colonel Comstock was killed. Sergeant Maltman has returned, which is some good news.

Here today is Christmas Day, but it don't seem so. The Chaplain had a Christmas service, which most of the company attended. A few carols were tried, but it wasn't the choir back home.

Everyone here prays that this will be the last Christmas surrounded by war. The rebels we see are losing spirit and hope. Major Swift, our regiment com-

I Hear the Bugle's Call

mander, congratulated us for our courage in facing the dangers and hardships and spoke of this winter being the last spent fighting the devils. We all hope he's right. I must end this as I hear the bugle's call. Merry Christmas to all.

                        Your loving son Daniel

                        Company E
                        3rd Brigade
                        1st Division
                        9th Corps
                        Army of the Tennessee

Here our company sees another Christmas come and go. Last Christmas we were in Virginia and now here in Tennessee. This past year I've traveled a lifetime of miles. I seen too much death and destruction. My family, like so many others, have sacrificed. Schuyler carries his wound and the Lord only knows the fate of Harrison. As we look to 1864 we can only pray that these sacrifices have not been in vain. As the day ends I hear the bugle's call once more, it has taken on a melancholy sound.

By the middle of January our regiment moved from Blaine's Crossroads to Strawberry Plains on the Holston River. Here the mail caught up with us and a fine letter arrived from Pastor Hoover.

An Angry Wind

Paint Creek
Monday, January 4, 1864

Dear Daniel,

I am writing to thank you for your last letter of the 20th ult. I also want to express my sympathy and those of the Congregation concerning Harrison's misfortune.

You and your family can be assured that our most devoted prayers are spoken daily for the safe return of your brother and men from our area who are in harm's way.

Schuyler had informed us about the events of your regiment and the heroic actions of you, Harrison, and your compatriots. We are very fortunate to have brave men such as you and Harrison defending our sacred flag and country.

We are very pleased to have Schuyler home to be with Lomira and the children. We also are grateful to him as we call on him often to explain the events of the war that we read weekly.

The ladies of the church are preparing a winter package of knitted items and homemade goods which we hope make the long days of winter more comfortable for you and the others.

Do not concern yourself about your loved ones at home as they are doing well and wish to see you and Harrison soon.

We know that Harrison is in God's care as we all are.

In God's Name,
Pastor Neal Hoover

Also, a fine letter from Schuyler arrived.

I Hear the Bugle's Call

Paint Creek
Monday, January 18, 1864

Dear Brother,

As I'm putting pen to paper the wind is blowing up a flurry of snow. So far, this winter had been pretty kind, but just recently old man winter has taken to providing us with more snow and cold than we'd prefer.

Pa shared your recent letter with Lomira and me. We are all glad that the siege has ended but we do of course fret over Harrison's safety. It's also good to hear of Sergeant Maltman's return. Pass on my good wishes to all the company men. I do miss not sharing their tales around a campfire.

I've passed the word around about Harrison in case some other family hears of him from their loved one. I do pray that he is alive, but should he be in a Richmond prison, that aint easing my mind.

Thomas, John, and I, are tending to your farm and the livestock are bearing up well. With so much snow Thomas has been knocking off the snow from your roof. I'm sure you'd rather not have a snowpile in your parlor.

I hear that the church ladies are preparing some winter baskets for you and the others. Lomira is the leader of the sewing circle.

I hope that should you be in winter quarters you can find the time to write. I'll end now with Pa's usual saying, "Keep your head down."

Schuyler

It's always good to hear from Schuyler as I know he truly understands what we are going through and can relate those feelings to the rest of the family.

Although the siege had ended, the rebels still were in close proximity, skirmishing between small units was a daily routine. The closer enemy was the lack of warm clothing and other basic supplies. With the gifts from home I was faring better than most who lacked socks, or decent shoes, or blankets.

Along with the lack of supplies came the ever increasing signs of poor health. I reckon it would astound the folks back home if they could hear an army camp awakening. Rather than the sounds of a rooster announcing the arrival of a new day, the soldier is awakened by the chaotic din of hundreds of soldiers coughing as if to welcome the sun.

Before the day's duty would consume most of my day I wrote to Schuyler.

Strawberry Plains, Tennessee
Saturday, February 6, 1864

Dear Schuyler,

I trust this letter finds all of you in good health and spirits. As for us here, this winter has hit hard.

Since the siege at Knoxville ended the Seventeenth has been on the move east of town as Longstreet's divisions continue to stay in the area. We draw picket duty about every three days with twelve hour shifts.

We aint as concerned about the rebels as we are about our own care. We aint had any recent clothing issue and many of the men are in serious need of basic items like shoes and pants. I heard some men say we look like we are at Valley Forge with General Washington.

Our rations are barely enough to get by and winter clothes aint been seen. I'm afraid these conditions are causing sickness to rise. The only comfort is knowing the rebels are heard to be worse off with no help on the way.

We're told our supplies will increase as soon as the weather allows the roads to be used by the wagons.
I'm as usual beholding to you and Thomas and John for looking after my farm. I would hate to see the condition of it if you boys weren't tending to it.

I Hear the Bugle's Call

I've been told by Captain Phillips that Harrison's condition has been changed from "missing" to "captured." From what he told me, one of the men from the Seventeenth who had also been captured escaped as they were being taken to Richmond. He found our lines and reported back to headquarters. He told them that he was with Harrison and four others. I'm going to try to find this man and see what else he can tell me. Pass this information along to everyone and try to keep everyone's spirits up. There still could be a prisoner exchange, or so we can pray for.

I'll be ending now as I hear the bugle's call once more today.

> Brother Daniel,
>
> Company E
> 17th Mich Vol Regiment
> 2nd Brigade
> 1st Division
> 9th Army Corps
> Army of the Ohio

In February our regiment moved to Mossy Creek as we heard more rumors of Confederates on the move.

Winter seems to bring out the evil in some of our men. The devil's liquor is usually the cause of a man's sinful behavior. Depending on the severity of the breach of conduct the punishment was a minor as wearing a barrel while on guard duty for destroying army property to "riding the horse" (a wooden beam) for drunkenness. It seems that for a few of the men no amount of embarrassment or pain would convince them to turn away from spirits.

Near the end of February I received two welcomed letters from brother John and from brother Schuyler.

An Angry Wind

Paint Creek,
Monday, February 22, 1864

Dear Brother Daniel,

We here at home pray that this letter find you safe and in good health.

Schuyler has shared the sad news that Harrison is probably being held as a prisoner. Although if true, it eases our minds that he is still in the land of the living, but, we realize, being a captive in a prison camp is no guarantee of being in a safe or healthy condition.

We are constantly searching the newspapers of any hopeful work of prisoner exchange which could bring him safely home.

Pa and Ma are of course worried beyond description regardless of Schuyler or my efforts to keep them hopeful. We all here are concerned this worry could be a troublesome weight on them.

The newspapers tell little of what goes on in Tennessee so, we count on your letters to keep us informed.

Schuyler, Thomas, and I will soon begin planning for the spring planting season. We hear corn and wheat prices are on the rise so seed will be a bit higher also. I'll let you know soon how many new calves have been added to your herd and lambs too.

I will end now with good wished sent by Emma and everyone here.

Brother John

I Hear the Bugle's Call

Paint Creek
Monday, February 29, 1864

Dear Brother Daniel,

I was pleased to get your letter of the 6th inst. Lomira and me are pleased that you are in good health. I hope that your winter quarters is as tolerable as possible for you and your tentmates. Pass along my good wishes to John Mason, James Masters, and of course Sergeant Maltman. I do hope he has recovered fully from his wound.

We here are saddened that Harrison has been declared a captive, but we pray his is being watched over by the Almighty.

I read in the newspaper about the siege at Knoxville and the supply problems. Hopefully, by the time this letter reaches you, the supply wagons are seen more often.

We also hear back home that Grant may be going east to command and your corps may follow. Should that happen, I'd say it could be a queer feeling to perhaps march through our old camp back in Virginia.

Winter back here has been a snowy one for sure. John and I can't wait to begin the spring work but that seems a long way off.

Lomira and the young ones are doing fine. The youngest, Perry, is sprouting up like a weed. Seems to grow an inch a day.

Ma and Pa are holding up well but, they are fretful over Harrison. We try to raise up their spirits but without good news, it aint always successful.

Lomira has been busy putting together a package of clothes and edibles which hopefully you see arriving soon. We are might proud of you and the local men as you keep up the defense of our flag.

I also wanted to mention that Lomira and I had Perry baptized last Sunday the 21st. Pastor Hoover conducted the service with a full congregation in attendance. The young one has been growing like a weed.

An Angry Wind

Until the next letter. Keep your head down.

Brother Schuyler

As March began our regiment had moved to Morristown, Tennessee, but on the 17th we were ordered to march to Knoxville. The march of 190 miles took us ten hard days. Along the way I did receive a most unexpected letter.

Cone, Michigan
Wednesday, March 2, 1864

Dear Corporal McFall,

I was pleased to receive your letter of the 12th inst. Your words were a comfort to me as you helped me understand the circumstances of Harrison's capture. I and your family share your constant concern over his safety.

We also pray for your safe return and for the return of all the brave men from home.

I must confess I try to keep as busy and my mind as occupied as possible with my school children so as not to sink into total despair.

But, I also know that with Harrison's strong Christian beliefs and character, no harm will come to him and we both will see him soon.

Please feel free to write to me directly if you have word of Harrison's condition.

Sincerely,
Miss Katie Welch

I was most taken by Miss Welch's words of kindness and support and I hope I have good news about Harrison to write her in the future. I had written to her a while back as I thought she deserved some words from me concerning Harrison's capture.

I Hear the Bugle's Call

The rumors of our corps moving back east were proven true as we left Kentucky at the end of March with the next stop being Cincinnati, Ohio. A long train trip east finally took us to Camp Parole near Annapolis, Maryland. In route I had time to write brother John to apprise him of my travels.

Nicholasville, Kentucky
Monday, March 28, 1864

Dear Brother John and Family,

As you can see, the Seventeenth Michigan is on the move again. We are currently camped here in central Kentucky on a rail line south of Lexington. And it seems the reason for the move is that the Ninth Army Corps is headed back to Virginia.

For the past two months our regiment has been chasing real rebels or rumors of them from Blaines Crossroads to Mossy Creek, to Strawberry Plains. Early March found us camped at Morristown, Tennessee.

Two weeks ago we had to march near on two hundred miles to Knoxville, which took us ten days of hard marching in mud, ice, and ruts. We've been told we are heading for Cincinnati, then by boat and railroad to Virginia. Back in January we were finally issued new clothes as our old rags weren't fit to wear no more. We also head that the Eighth Michigan reenlisted, which earned them a furlough home. I do certainly want to travel back to see all of you but not for the price of any more years in this army.

I've had no more word about Harrison. He's a strong boy and we can only pray that he gets exchanged soon.

I felt it my duty to write to his friend, Katie Welch back in Cone. I tried to put her at ease about Harrison's capture. I know he felt strongly about her and I hope she'll keep her spirits up.

As March is ending so is winter down here. The daylight lingers and the trees are budding. Winter down here is a bit more tolerable than back home.

I continue to receive letters from Pastor Hoover and I write him back when I can. It's good to know we here are still thought of by family and friends.

Your preparations for the spring planting season makes me a bit jealous. Although I can sure recall the hours of toiling behind my team, I'd trade that job for this for sure.

With all of this traveling I'm not sure how well the mail will keep up but, I still look forward to reading your letters and the newspapers sent this way. I must end now as I am in charge of our company pickets.

                    Your brother Daniel,

                    Company E
                    17th Mich Vol Regiment
                    2nd Brigade
                    1st Division
                    9th Army Corps
                    Army of the Ohio

Our regiment received two-hundred new recruits at Annapolis and we welcomed them as we were once welcomed by referring to them as "fresh fish."

Now that we are back east we have been reunited with the Army of the Potomac. Although General Burnside remains our corps commander, our overall commander is General Meade with General Grant looking over his shoulder. A few of the men wonder how this "pecking order" will play out but, as a lowly Corporal that question is not one I care to concern myself with.

As we have arrived here in the east so has spring. The trees are in bloom and the songbirds' calls are a welcome sound. But with spring we know comes more battles, more death. I find our company's spirits remain high and our cause remains worth the fight. But I also know that soon the songs of the birds will be replaced by the echoes of cannons and the hellish sounds of battle. I can hardly remember a time before August of 1862. As Harrison has been captured, perhaps in a strange way I have too.

I Hear the Bugle's Call

That Distant, Quiet Place
April 1864 – July 1864

On the morning of April 23rd after receiving some new men our corps rode the cars to Washington and marched back through the city. As we marched past the President's house we happened to spy Mr. Lincoln getting into his carriage. We halted our march and when he spied our regiment's flag he came to the gate to greet us. Company E of course could not let this occasion slip by and we began to sing, "The Battle Cry of Freedom." The President seemed to enjoy our small serenade. At the finish, he complimented our voices and our corps efforts in Tennessee. We then took up our march and as we proceeded down the street the echoes of "John Brown's Body" trailed from our company.

We continued our way out of town until we reached Warrenton Junction. There we reunited with the Army of the Potomac.

When we set up camp I was pleased to see that the mail had caught up with us. I had received welcomed letters from John, Schuyler, and a surprised note from Louis Haner.

I Hear the Bugle's Call

Paint Creek
Tuesday, April 12, 1864

Dear Daniel,

We were pleased to receive your letter of March. We have read that the Ninth Corps was heading back east to hook up with the Army of the Potomac once more. We can only pray that with the coming of spring, peace also arrives.
I trust you'd be happy to hear that three calves have been born to add to your herd. Also, four lambs have been added to your flock. Thomas and I are about to begin the shearing. We haven't heard what the going rate is this year but with the war, prices for most farm goods have risen.

Schuyler and I are done with our maple tree tapping. We aren't through boiling it down but we figure to get a good price in Ypsilanti for the syrup.
I'm glad you wrote to Miss Welch. From what Ma and our sisters tell me, she is a fine young woman and is quite worried about Harrison. Of course we all share that concern.

You mentioned that you missed the spring chores. I too wish you could share our "pleasure" in being hitched to the team.

I will finish now as storm is brewing and I need to check on your livestock and mine.

Write when you can.

John and family

That Distant, Quiet Place

Paint Creek
Saturday April 23, 1864

Dear Daniel,

I hope this letter finds you safe sitting by a fire with a full cooking pot. We here back home are doing well.

Spring has finally arrived and with John and Thomas, we have begun the spring work. We've tapped the maples, and are about to start plowing as the fields have about dried enough.

I suppose you haven't heard anything more about Harrison. We can only hope he's getting humane treatment by the rebels. With no word for this length of time, it's been very hard on all.

While John and I were over tending to your farm we came across Louis Haner. With his farm next to yours he's been helping us keep an eye on it. I told him you might like to hear from someone other than family. He said he'd get to writing soon.

Our young ones are as active as a litter of puppies. They seem to grow an inch a week. We read that you and the men are back in Virginia. I know with spring, comes more battles. Perhaps with Grant and Meade commanding, this ungodly conflict ends soon.

Pastor Hoover tells me he and you exchange letters. He's a fine man who really cares about the men defending our flag.

I'll end now as night has fallen. Keep your head down!

Brother Schuyler

I Hear the Bugle's Call

Paint Creek
Monday, April 25, 1864

Dear Daniel,

I would bet that you are quite surprised by getting a letter from me. I was talking to your brother John while he was over at your place. He said you'd probably like to hear from other folks beside family and I told him I might send a letter your way.

Schuyler and John keep me informed about how you and the others from the area are doing. I of course was sorry to hear about Harrison's capture. He is a fine young man and all of us are praying for his safe return.

Your brothers are doing a fine job keeping up your place and I don't mind lending a hand when needed.

Last month I finally cleared the brush pile that was overgrown along where my pasture ran near your stream. I've killed a passel of muskrats whose homes were in that brush.

We read about your regiment heading back east. Schuyler is our military source for questions. He seems to be getting along well with his injury.

I'll end now as this letter is the most I've written in years. We here are proud of what you men are doing for our country.

Respectfully,
Louis Haner

During the month we also received our pay which was a welcomed event. As we were camped at a place called Camp Parole our rations improved now that we were closer to the supply depot. We were also refitted with everything from socks to tents. All of these changes were well received but we also knew that the call of the bugle to face the enemy would not be long in coming. We guessed that fighting under General Grant might be different than General

Burnside, but would the difference bring on final victory?

These quieter camp days allowed me to catch up on my letter writing as I penned a long past due letter to my parents.

Warrenton Junction, Virginia
Monday, May 1, 1864

Dear Parents and Sisters,

I would assume everyone at home is surprised to finally get a letter from me. I know I haven't written since Christmas and I apologize for that. I assume the letters I send to Schuyler and John get passed around to all.

The Ninth Corps has been here in Virginia for almost two months. We are part of the Army of the Potomac led by General Meade with General Grant nearby. General Burnside is still our corps commander.

We left Alexandria and arrived here at Warrenton Junction today. When we first got to Washington our regiment marched passed the President's house. Mr. Lincoln was about to get in his carriage when he saw our regiment march near the gate. We halted and as he came forward to greet us, we in Company E started up in song. You folks should have heard us sing out "The Battle Cry of Freedom." The President stood there smiling and seemed to enjoy it. When we finished he told us he hasn't heard that well a tune sung for quite some time. As we started up marching we began a favorite of ours, "John Brown's Body."

As we marched to our present position we passed over the old Bull Run battlefield. It would tear at your heart to see the remains of such brave men exposed to the elements from the shallow graves. It aint fitting treatment for brave men.

As the month of May begins so will the season of fighting and marching.

General Grant seems to be a man who doesn't scare easy. Our country may have finally found the equal to General Lee.

I still hold out for Harrison's safe return. We must continue to think of a happier day when we are all together again.

I must end now as the bugle calls for an inspection of the regiment. Please send envelopes and stamps.

                    Your son and brother

                    Daniel,
                    Company E
                    1st Brigade
                    3rd Division
                    9th Corps
                    Army of the Potomac

These quiet days too quickly ended as our corps began marching south through the old Bull Run battlefield. We couldn't help seeing and nearly tripping over skeleton remains of men who had died earlier and now seem to rise up out of their shallow graves. I could see as our company passed these scenes, the look on the men's faces. Most could not hide their shock as they spied skulls and arms that seemed to reach up to heaven for salvation.

Our corps was assigned to follow the rest of the men as a separate unit led by General Burnside. Following an army on the march means eating a stomach full of dust as thousands of feet and hooves churn up the dusty roads. Our clean uniforms as well as our dry throats paid the price.

We crossed the Rapidan River and camped near a plantation. As soon as the order came to halt for the night I, as corporal, had to assist Sergeant Maltman in organizing the tent layout and assign men for picket duty. With the enemy known to be in the vicinity picket duty took on its most serious aspects as sharpshooters were always a possibility.

Our regiment lay in reserve during the day and evening of May 5th. Early in the morning of the 7th we were ordered to the front and engaged the rebels a little before noon.

Somehow I survived this action and two days later wrote a letter home to Schuyler with what little strength I could muster.

Near Spottsylvania, Virginia
Monday, May 9, 1864

Dear Schuyler,

I am writing this as the day is ending an as some tiring and confusing days have taken place.

On Wednesday, the Ninth corps began marching south from Manassas. Our corps under General Burnside acts as a separate unit from the other corps under General Meade and General Grant.

Our march was a hard one as we were to follow the rest of the Army of the Potomac which kicked up clouds of dust ahead of us. We crossed the Rapidan River near the Chancellorsville battlefield.

This morning we were camped near a plantation called Spotswood. Word came to us that our task was for our division along with Colonel Potter's Second division to flank the rebels on their right.

We rose early and started out but the route was a mess. We ran into the rear of the Sixth corps with all of their wagons, horses, and troops blocking one narrow roadway. The congestion was finally cleared and around 5 o'clock in the morning. We stopped near a place called Wilderness Tavern.

Firing was heard in the distance as the Second and Third Divisions advanced along a narrow lane. We halted near a store. Here we received orders to break ranks and prepare our breakfasts. This order was welcomed after two days of hard marching but still a little surprising as we still heard fighting off in the distance. We soon met rebel pickets and brisk artillery fire started coming down around us like hail. Orders were then given to change direction and head south. We were now to march till we reached the Second Corps flank. Our brigade and Colonel Potter's division found the going near impossible. We had to traverse through pine thickets, swamps and brush. We could barely see the sky. The echo of battle seemed to come from everywhere. Not a lane or road or even a cowpath to be seen. We finally broke through around 3 pm. We reached what was believed to be General Longstreet's flank. The day had turned unbearably hot and most of our canteens were near dry.

We came upon the enemy behind makeshift breastworks of trees and brush. Our regiment was held in reserve but only for a short while. Col. Hartranft sent the 2nd, 8th and the 17th Michigan to meet the enemy.

Our gain was slowed and it appeared that a kind of draw took place. Neither side would give so no advantage was achieved.

By about 6 p.m. the fighting had about ended. I guess the men on both sides were just too tired, hungry, and thirsty to keep at it.

We are now to stay at our posts and get what rest we can. It has been a confusing day. Sgt. Maltman and I agree that when fighting in a place like this there can't be any winners. We're told this area is called the Wilderness. I'd say that name is dead-on.

> Brother Daniel
> Company E
> 1st Brigade
> 3rd Division
> 9th Corps
> Army of the Potomac

We crossed the Nye River on the ninth and found the enemy ready to meet us.

We were temporarily detached from the First Brigade to support a New York Battery, we moved ahead at the doublequick and up a hill at which an Ohio

Regiment had been repulsed.

We arrived at the hill just ahead of the rebels who were charging up the other side. We stopped them in their tracks with a well concentrated volley. The rebels fell back leaving us in command of the hill. We continued trading fire with rebels on the 10th and 11th days of May.

As the sun rose on the morning of the 12th, I doubt anyone else could have known what events would place before that late spring sunlight would fade into night.

We awoke early and ate our biscuits cold as no fires were allowed. The regiment was on the extreme left of the Union line. Our brigade was led by Colonel Hartranft. I, and the rest of the regiment spent the morning enduring the fire of the enemy's artillery and skirmishes as well as moving through fog and light rain. A miserable start to the day to say the least. Our brigade consisted of the Second, Eighth and Twenty-seventh Michigan Regiments, as well as the 109th New York and the Fifty-First from Pennsylvania. Sergeant Maltman was in the lead of myself and 15 from our company. As we approached the enemy's works, we saw rebels on our left as they seemed to appear magically from the fog and mist.

Then we heard the rebels' yell, that sound which we've heard on other battlefields that can only mean we're in for a fight. James Masters shouted, "Look to the rear!" and with that warning came the rebels as it appeared they had us penned in like a flock of sheep. John Yaw, James Masters, Sergeant Maltman, and I fired our rifles, then with our bayonets and rifle butts took on the rebels nearest to our position.

After a short time that seemed like hours, we heard the bugle sound retreat. As we attempted to reform to the rear Sergeant Maltman and James Masters separated from John Yaw and me.

In the confusion of the mist, fog, and smoke, of battle I happened to come up to a rebel officer from behind. I hadn't reloaded my rifle due to the rebels buzzing around us like bees. I therefore pointed my bayonet at the back of his tattered, dusty, gray coat and with a voice barely heard over the battle I shouted, "Sir, drop your weapon while you still have life!" he quickly froze in place and while turning towards me his sidearm fell to the ground. I could see his uniform bore the rank of colonel as he bowed his head in compliance. John Yaw and I led our prisoner towards our lines and as we made our way around a tangled mass of thorn bushes we came upon two rebels holding a Federal officer. Our sudden appearance got their attention and immediately I demanded that our colonel order those men to surrender with their prisoner. The two men were so shocked at seeing us they quickly obeyed the command and threw down their rifles. I and John just looked at each other and shook our heads in disbelief of what we've just accomplished.

We made it back to our lines of earlier in the day, and with a bit of pride we released our prisoners to the first Provost Officer we came across. We were told that snaring an officer would mark us for promotion. But John and I agreed we'd settle for a full canteen and the shade of a tree.

As the sun began to set on that Thursday, the battle also faded. Company E and the Seventeenth Michigan took a powerful beating. As we reformed, the number of casualties stunned all of us. At least thirteen of our company were missing including my close friends Sergeant Maltman and James Masters. Colonel Luce and Major Swift were also missing as the regimental losses were tallied. And my friend, Herbert Lounsbury, was killed as he ran to recapture our Regimental Flag. The wounded and dead laid on the field as any attempt to come to their aid resulted in sharpshooters adding to the toll. How awful it was to hear the calls of the suffering as they pleaded for water or loved ones. Finally exhaustion won out and sleep finally came to me as night took control of the battlefield.

The Seventeenth's flag was lost although more an one man braved bullets and shrapnel to carry our flag forward.

I found out later that our captured rebel colonel was a Colonel Barbour of the Thirty-seventh North Carolina Regiment. The Federal officer who we "convinced" the rebels to release, was Lieutenant Harmon from our regiment.

The days after the battle were taken up with resupply and as an uneasy stalemate played out over the battlefield. Our corps didn't rest long as on Friday we were ordered to form up as the Army of the Potomac began moving east and south. A river called the North Anna was to be crossed. I and John Yaw agreed that General Grant is a different kind of commander. Under General McClellan or Burnside a fight like we just had would have been followed by days or weeks of inaction. But General Grant aint one for sittin still regardless of the situation. To him it's "keep moving!"

Crossing the North Anna wasn't going to be a frolic. In fact, General Lee and his forces put up a strong showing as the Seventeenth Michigan was involved in small skirmishes. The rebel stand was determined enough to cause General Grant to revise this plan and we again picked ourselves up and headed east. The continued loss of men was highly regrettable. The picket fire and sharpshooting along the North Anna was deadly. There was an unwritten code of honor among the infantry that forbade shooting of men while attending to calls of nature. Men from both sides violated the code.

On the 16th of May I finally had the time and relative comfort to write a letter home to Schuyler informing him about the month's action.

Spottsylvania, Virginia
Monday, May 16, 1864

Dear Schuyler,

To say our regiment has again been in a real fight would be a mighty strong understatement. If you have received my letter of the 9th in it you've read about the battle in the wilderness of a week or so back. But what we've been through just four days ago makes the former tussle seem like a church picnic.

I Hear the Bugle's Call

Since the 8th of May our division had moved south through the old Chancellorsville battlefield to near Spotsylvania Court House where we found the rebels dug in.

The 2nd brigade had encountered a defiant enemy and our regiment was ordered forward to attack, and we attacked the rebels flank. With a stout determination we drove the rebels from the field. General Wilcox commended our regiment's courage by giving us the key position of our line to hold, that being on the left.

On the 12th the Third division advanced driving the enemy back. About mid-day we were ordered to again advance which we did under heavy enemy fire. We had no more covered about eighty rods when out of a mist and fog our regiment became encircled by the rebels. They came at us an soon John Maltman, John Yaw, and I were defending ourselves with our bayonets, rifle butts and fists.

As we were trying to move back, John Maltman was cornered by three rebels and had to surrender. John Yaw and I continued and as we did I came up from behind a rebel Colonel and with my bayonet pointing at his throat he decided to surrender. While moving through the smoke and fog we came to a couple of rebels holding one of our officers. I ordered our captured colonel to demand the rebels surrender with their captain. We thus bagged a gang of rebels and saved Lieutenant Barker; a Union officer.

We made it back to the rear where we then found a Provost Officer who accepted our prisoners. By near sundown the fighting had ended and we all were plenty tired.

I heard that our regimental colors were captured and Edwin Bush tells me that Sergeant Maltman, and Captain Phillips, and Major Swift were all captured. Lieutenant Knight now commands our company. The casualty list confirms what I can see around me. This company has had a severe beating but we held and gave as good as we got.

Earlier today the 17th was assigned to General Willcox Headquarters guard.

It seems that until we get our numbers back to strength, we may not see much fighting. We could all use some rest.

I must admit, these days of fighting and escaping death by a cat's whisker has had a life changing effect on my. More than once when the battle is raging and ear shattering noises are all around, a feeling comes over me. It's like as I am charging the enemy, the man in front of me is in my way. He becomes an obstacle along my search, the search for that distant, quiet place, a place where I can rest, a place to look around and see life, not death.

I hear the bugle's call, so I must end for now. Give everyone my best regards and tell Ma and Pa not to worry none.

> Brother Daniel,
>
> Co. E
> 17th Mich. Vol Rgt
> Acting Engineers
> 3rd Division
> 9th Corps
> Army of the Potomac

Early in the afternoon of the 16th Lieutenant Knight, who was our acting company commander, as Captain Phillips was missing in battle, called a company formation to tell us that our regiment was being reassigned to new duties as our roster had been so decimated during the month

This news was certainly unexpected. What was left of our company was but a handful. I heard that our regiment's numbers were down to less than company level.

We were marched to the rear and reported to General Willcox's Headquarters. His adjutant read us an order that stated, due to our company's courage, determination, and ability, our regiment will be reassigned." We found out soon that our new assignment would be as pioneers working on building

I Hear the Bugle's Call

bridges or fortifications, or at times, as provost guards. My first thought was we were being punished for doing our duty. We had fought from Maryland to Tennessee, to Virginia, and now our effort wasn't needed. But after talking with John Yaw and others, I came to look at the situation differently. We've certainly done our duty, we've shown our will to fight and now until we gain numbers back to a full regiment, we can defend our flag in other ways.

The end of May brought on a huge battle near a place called Cold Harbor. The Seventeenth Michigan saw little action as again General Grant and General Lee locked horns. Our forces came out of the fight severely bloodied but again rather than retreat, the Army of the Potomac headed south toward a Confederate railhead at Petersburg.

Our regiment had the task of repairing the fortifications around the Ninth Corps' positions. It sure seemed strange, almost like being home as I worked with shovel and axe. Although if I were at home, I would have no need for a rifle within arm's reach.

By mid June we had reached the area around Petersburg which would be our position for we hoped not long. The mail again reached our camp and a welcomed letter from Schuyler arrived.

> Paint Creek
> Tuesday, May 31, 1964

Dear Brother Daniel,

I wanted to respond to you as soon as I received your letters of the 8th and 16th inst.

We have read some of what you've told us in the newspapers. But we know what we read about always to be believed as fact.

By your telling it sure sounds like you've been through more than your share of tight fixes. All of us thank the Lord for your safe keeping. I so wish I could be with you and the boys to help out our company when the thunder begins.

Ma and Pa are worried as usual but reading them your letters have put their minds to ease for a spell.

I'm sorry to hear about Sergeant Maltman and James Masters being captured. Perhaps they will come by Harrison and they all can look out for each other. And perhaps the loss of our colors will only be a temporary setback. The strong reputation of our regiment means a whole lot more than a piece of cloth anyways.

Your capturing of a rebel colonel and saving one of our officers has been big news around this area. I sure would like to have seen the look on that old rebel's face as he stared at the cold steel held by a determined McFall.

Lomira, Emma, and the church ladies have another package of supplies and food being readied for shipment to you and the boys. The corn is looking good as we have had some spring rains and sun. Your herd has three new calves which are doing just fine and your wood fetched a decent price.

I will write more when I can.

Brother Schuyler

While most of the time we were put to work erecting ammunition depots and siege fortifications, we at times were called out as skirmishers testing the rebels' positions as both sides dug into the landscape like gophers. Our regiment was involved in an attack on the Norfolk and Petersburg Railroad as we attempted to cut off one of the rebel's supply routes. I was part of a force made up of three companies. We did succeed in tearing up a mile or so of track while taking a few casualties. Fortunately, my men and I had luck on our side as we returned to camp unscathed and bringing in two rebel prisoners.

Chaplain Greene conducted a fine Sabbath service and afterwards our mail call brought me a fine letter from Pastor Hoover and my parents.

I Hear the Bugle's Call

Paint Creek
Thursday, June 16, 1864

Dear Daniel,

Schuyler has informed us recently of the intense fighting you and the other men of the area have participated in. Everyone here at the church gives thanks to the Lord for you and your comrades safe keeping. We have been reading in the newspapers about the battles going on in Virginia with heightened interest.

We all are so very proud of the courage and devotion to our nation's cause you men display.

Our prayers go out to the families of the departed and wounded as well as the captured such as the Masters family. As the fighting increases so must the prayers.

Our Women's Aid Society are again organizing some boxes of clothing and food items which hopefully you and the others will see and enjoy soon.

Daniel, you have a loving and devoted family who have looked out for your farm and livestock with great care.

We all hope to see you, Harrison and the other brave men return home soon, safe under God's care.

Sincerely,
Pastor Neal Hoover

That Distant, Quiet Place

Cone, Michigan
Monday, June 13, 1864

Dear Daniel,

All here at home pray that this letter finds you safe and healthy.

Schuyler has kept us informed of your actions which I must admit cause us no small amount of anxiety and worry. But Schuyler reminds us that you are a very capable soldier and with God's grace, will survive to return to us.

John and Pa are busy with getting the sickle, and the hay rake ready for the three acres of clover that's about ready.

Your sisters send their best as us womenfolk are busy with our kitchen garden.

Pastor Hoover stopped by last week to see how everyone was and stayed for supper. A good man he is. There was an article in the Monroe Times about the battle at Spottsylvania. They listed the men of the 17th Regiment who were captured or were casualties. Our hearts were pounding as we anxiously read the names. Our nerves calmed as your name wasn't included. We were happily surprised to read a short account of the bravery shown by some of the men of Company E including a Corporal McFall! How thrilled we are of your bravery and others in defense of our country. We continue to pray for Harrison's safe return.

I will end now as your Pa and John are due in for supper. Take care and write when you can.

With love,
Ma and Pa

On Monday, July 4th we celebrated our country's independence. Last July our regiment was camped outside of Vicksburg. Today we're dug in outside of another rebel encampment. War for us began as a struggle fought over fields and valleys, but has become a battle of physical and mental endurance as both sides have dug miles of trenches. Men dare not stand up or show themselves if they treasure life. I now have no regrets about being reassigned to the rear. Most of us in my tent don't care to live each day like a gopher afraid of the next shot. I wrote a letter to John describing our new assignment and near the end of July I received a first rate letter from brother John.

Petersburg, Virginia
Monday, July 4, 1864

Dear Brother John,

Here is another Independence Day. Last year our regiment was outside of Vicksburg, Mississippi and this year encamped near Petersburg, Virginia. Although it's been only one year it seems like a lifetime.

You have no doubt heard from Schuyler of the events that took place here in Virginia since May. Somehow I came through the storms of battle but many good men didn't such as John Maltman, Captain Delos Phillips, and too many others who were captured. We regret the loss of Herbert Lonsberry, Peter Doftsch, Michal Harrigan, and Alex Jack, all good men. Those men should always be honored.

Since the battles of May our regiment was assigned provost duty and occasionally pioneer duty. Provost duty usually consists of guarding prisoners (of which we have a large number of) or standing around trying to look alert as we guard Colonel Willcox and other officers. Prisoner watching consists of guarding rebels as they are herded into stock pens. You wouldn't believe the condition of these men. Most are barefoot, dirty, and clothed in the most ragged forms of uniforms. It amazes one to think why are they and their leaders still defiant and headstrong.

What we've seen of the southern people their lives are as downtrodden as their soldiers. We haven't been too occupied as pioneers except for tearing up a few miles of rebel railroad track. That work beats toting a rifle first rate.

I've heard from Ma and Pa and Schuyler and that brings a good feeling to my mind. I suppose the July heat has come on back home as it surely has here.

Our supply depot is at a place called White House Landing and finally we are seeing better rations and clean uniforms. Also, mail seems to have found us, as has the paymaster.

Tell everyone I'm thinking of them and not to worry none. Company E aint near the front, though a stray shell is always a threat to visit.

I must end as I hear the bugle's call.

>Daniel,
>Co. E
>17th Mich Vol Regiment
>Acting Engineers
>3rd Division
>9th Corps
>Army of the Potomac

I Hear the Bugle's Call

Paint Creek
Wednesday, July 20, 1864

Brother Daniel,

I received your letter of the 4th inst. We all are relieved and grateful to the Almighty for your safe well-being.

The newspapers have mentioned the fighting in Virginia and we scour the lists of casualties hoping not to find your name and others from home. It certainly seems that with all the fighting, the confederacy can't keep their stubborn rebellion for much longer. Is there any chance of a break for you so you could come home awhile? We have seen some men who have gotten a few days furlough and return. It would be a first rate surprise for all of us to see you walking up the road.

Schuyler, Thomas, and I have been working your farm and although we could use some rain your corn is looking fine. The wheat on Schuyler's farm and mine brought in 25 cents a bushel and the yield was more than last season.

Your orchard came through the spring in fine shape. The apple trees appear full. I may have a deal for one of your heifers. Louis Haner has a need for one and if I can get him to offer up his extra hay rake, we might strike a deal.

Emma and the young ones are doing well, and also help look after your place.

I do worry about Ma and Pa, as they are showing their age more. But, of course they say, "don't fret about us none, the McFall clan don't age, we improve!" And so they go on.

Pastor Hoover continues to lead us in prayer on the Sabbath for you and the others.

Take care and write when you can.

John

I do so envy my brothers at home working the soil. At times in the evening, I close my eyes, and I can see my farm with corn knee high in the east ten acres, and Paint Creek flowing near by. I will survive this devil's game of war and return home.

Early on the morning of Saturday, the 30th, I and my tentmates were jolted awake by a nearby explosion. It felt like the earth had exploded. It had the sound like the roar of a bear charging from a cave.

What could this be? An accident back at the ammunition depot? A real earthquake? Perhaps a rebel attempt to break free of our lines. I ran out the tent not knowing what I might find.

I Hear the Bugle's Call

The Last Bugle Has Sounded
August 1864 – June 1865

The earth had exploded, but due to man, not nature. Captain Phillips, who had returned to our company after being exchanged, called a company assembly and passed on the news that a Federal mine had been detonated under the rebel fortification.

The plan was to have some former miners from a Pennsylvania regiment dig a shaft under the rebels and place over 400 kegs of gunpowder at the end. When the explosion took place Federal troops would rush into the crater and exploit the chaos and take control of the rebel lines.

As we found out later the plan was a total failure. Many of our troops became trapped and were easily killed or captured. This crater blunder is just another example of the poor planning that leads to the callous loss of life that has gone on for both armies for much too long.

Early in August mail call was kind to me as I received a welcomed letter from Schuyler.

Paint Creek
Tuesday, August 4, 1864

Dear Brother Daniel,

We here at home pray this letter finds you and your companions safe and in fine health. John has shared with the family your letter of July.

I am relieved that your company has been assigned safer duty, but I understand that the reassignment was due to the loss of many good men.

Any word on Harrison or Sergeant Maltman? I continue to try to keep our family's hopes up for our dear brother's safe return. But privately, I am becoming more inclined to think of the chances of that reunion being very small. Back here, the summer heat is on with a dry spell of the last two weeks. Your corn still looks first rate and Thomas and I brought in a fine crop of hay from your east five acres.

The young ones are busy with their pets and Elenora has taken to kitchen chores right smart. We read about General Burnside being replaced by General Parke. I always felt Burnside was a good and decent man. From what I read some of his colleagues weren't so convinced of his soldiering skills. But you're the expert now. What's your feelings on the man? We also are reading a lot about the Presidential election coming on soon. I can't believe our country would turn its back on "old Abe" while the war goes on and especially for "Little Mac." I fear that if the Democrats win, the cause that so many have fought and died for will be surrendered. But that's my mind's notions. I'll end as its time for bed.

Take care and keep your head down.

Schuyler

General Parke had replaced General Burnside, who was heading back to Rhode Island. We were told he was needed back home to help reelect the President. He had been getting a lot of negative opinions from the newspaper reporters that flock around our camp. He is a good man and to my way of thinking was a capable commander of our corps. I must say, General Parke seems to be a good replacement. I hope he leads our corps to the end of this nightmare soon.

As the month of September came upon us, our regiment gained new men. The draft had provided some much needed recruits. I expressed my idea that we need all the "fresh fish" that comes our way be they volunteer or "be volunteered."

Later in the month I was surprised as I was promoted with another stripe. Captain Phillips called me out of the line during a roll call and pulls out a sergeant's chevron. He read an order that promoted me due to that "dog fight" of a battle back in May. To top it off I got a raise in pay to $17.00 a month.

The Last Bugle Has Sounded

I also knew that the money came attached to more duties as a non-commissioned officer. With this news I wrote home to brother Schuyler.

Near Poplar Springs, Virginia
Wednesday, September 28, 1864

Dear Schuyler,

I received your last letter with much appreciation and interest. I haven't been writing often as our regiment has been kept busy jumping from one place to another as the Army of the Potomac tries to tighten the noose around General Lee and his forces outside of Petersburg.

Our regiment now numbers about ninety with the adding of some twelve recruits earlier in the month. It pains me to think of the number that left Detroit and now to see what we now call a regiment. I have not heard anything about our dear brother, and I also fear for his well being. We must continue to pray and have faith that He will guide him home. I do have some news that may surprise you. Just two days ago I was promoted to sergeant! I guess my fight back at Spottsylvania made someone up the command ladder think I warranted another stripe. With that stripe comes a raise to $17.00 a month and a haversack full of new duties. Andrew Kelly was also promoted to sergeant.

Captain Phillips has returned to command Company E. He had been captured back in May. I do bring sad news as our friend Edwin Bush died in June. He had been shot by a sharpshooter while sitting with his comrades talking about his Vicksburg expedition. He died of a head wound. He was a fine Christian and a brave soldier.

General Parke has replaced Burnside as you read. We hear General Burnside is going back to Rhode Island to help get Mr. Lincoln reelected.

The Presidential talk has been a major campfire topic. Most of the men here don't have much stock in "Little Mac" winning. I, like you, don't want to see the sacrifices we all have made given up for a peace that allows the South a victory.

I Hear the Bugle's Call

The regiment continues to work mainly as pioneers building fortifications and occasionally guarding prisoners. We've been called out as reserves but haven't seen any large action so far. This siege seems to have no end. I can't believe the rebels can hold out much longer. Hopefully we can go home by the new year. I'll end now as I hear the bugle's call for assembly.

> Brother Daniel,
>
> Company E
> Acting Engineers,
> 1st Division
> 9th Corps
> Army of the Potomac

One advantage of being near the rear is that we are close to the support of the Sanitary Commission. The men and women volunteers who at times have found themselves in the path of the fighting have been a Godsend. I have seen them helping in the field hospitals or walking through camp offering coffee, cakes or other needed items such as stamps, envelopes or pocket Bibles. During the month of October our regiment was involved in a few small skirmishes at such unknown places such as; Hatcher's Run, Boyton Plank Road, and Squirrel Level Road. Each of these was attempts by us to cut off the rebels supplies and tighten their noose a bit more. No major casualties resulted, but at this stage of the war any loss of life or wounding of men is beyond reason.

Earlier in the month I received a fine letter from Pastor Hoover. After which I responded in kind.

The Last Bugle Has Sounded

Paint Creek
Thursday, October 13, 1964

Dear Daniel,

I write this letter with faith that you are safe and in good spirits. Your letter of the 5th inst. was greatly welcomed.

We, in the congregation, are immensely interested in the news. Schuyler and John share with us concerning your activities as well as the other brave men of your regiment.

We are greatly thankful for your survival during those terrible days back in May. We do share sorrow over the death of Herbert Lounsbury and the capture of James Masters. We continue to pray for their safe return, and of course, also for Harrison's safety.

Your brothers and Thomas continue their devoted supervision of your farm. Mrs. Hoover has been working with Lomira and Emma to knit socks and collect food items for you and the men. I'm very proud of our church women for their tireless efforts to help all of our brave men.

As the season of fall comes upon us we pray for an end to the ungodly conflict.

Be assured He marches with you.

Pastor Neal Hoover

Before the month was over Delos Phillips resigned and went back to Michigan. He certainly earned our respect and I believe his treatment while being held captive may have led to his resignation. Lieutenant Knight is our company commander at least for now. He did a good job earlier when Captain Phillips had been captured.

October ran into November with some news arriving from home.

I Hear the Bugle's Call

Paint Creek
Friday, November 4, 1864

Dear Daniel,

I apologize for not getting back to you sooner after receiving your fine letter last month. But as I'm sure you know this time of the year is a mighty busy one.

The weather wasn't helpful as the rains kept us out of the cornfields until mid October. My acreage that runs near your south ten yielded a tolerable amount.

I was talking to Thomas and John as they were picking your crop and they let on that you were keeping busy there in Virginia. They said you would be in winter quarters waiting out for spring. We are all praying this devilish war was played out by then.

A fall wind storm tore some shingles off your barn, but John and I were able to nail down some new ones, no harm done.

Keep hoping that Schuyler would give me some good news about Harrison, but we can only keep praying for that day to come.

I'll be ending now so keep safe.

Louis

It is always a welcome sight to read from friends from back home. Louis is a good friend and neighbor, I'll try to repay him in some way when I return.

November brought on some colder winds and a Presidential election. William Winegar of Grass Lake was an election commissioner who came from Michigan to oversee the regiment's vote. He had been a former officer in the regiment.

The Last Bugle Has Sounded

Each man was called from formation and entered a tent to cast his vote. It brought on a feeling of being back home as each man had the chance to cast his ballot. Most men said they felt like this was the soldier's turn to speak up on the war. Without any reservation I cast my vote for Mr. Lincoln and Mr. Johnson, General McClellan had some good qualities as our commander but if he's going to stand on his party's surrender of this war, he's not my President. Later we were told our regiment voted 146 for Mr. Lincoln and 48 for General McClellan. I'd say the soldier's voice has spoken.

Most of our company rejoiced when we heard Mr. Lincoln had earned the country's support for another term. This war can't last much longer and with the "Railsplitter" still astride his horse, the country is on the right path.

Winter quarters is tolerable as the Ninth Corps has shifted a bit but still astride Petersburg. Colonel Luce had returned to lead the regiment back in October, but due to poor health he resigned and Lieutenant Colonel Swift took command as November was coming to a close.

Reveille sounded at exactly 5 a.m. on the morning of Monday the 19th of December. After the usual meal of bacon, biscuits and coffee that would dissolve a horseshoe. I organized a work detail of ten men for the day. We were ordered to replace some telegraph posts that the rebel calvary had shut down behind the Ninth Corps position.

As I was about to march out with my men, I was surprised by a most unexpected voice. From behind I hear, "Well, what has this army come to, this man I see is now a sergeant." With that assertion ringing in my ears I turn and who do I spy but my old tentmate John Maltman!

We immediately grabbed each other's shoulders and then a hearty handshake followed. Much to my surprise he had on a First Lieutenant's bars on his shoulders. He noticed my expression and quickly stated that during his capture he had been promoted should he return, and was assigned to Company H. Knowing I was still needed for pioneer duty, I asked Sergeant Kelly to take my place, which he did.

John and I then had the time to it down with a cup of coffee as he told me a most startling and I must say, heart rendering account as Harrison's fate became known. I listened intently as Maltman began his tale.

He and many other Federals had been captured during the fighting on May 12th at Spottsylvania. As he and others were marched to the rear of the rebel's camp he spied General Lee. They marched about three miles then stopped for the night. More Federal captives were added until the group numbered possibly one thousand or more.

They spent a rainy night and received no rations for two days, and then meager amounts of flour and bacon.

Eventually he and the others marched then halted at Gordonsville where the guards robbed them of anything thought to be of value. He had a pocket watch, money, and his shoes taken from him. A pocket Bible was the only possession not confiscated.

They were packed in box cars, twice as many as the car should hold so not everyone could sit. They took turns sitting and standing by the half open door where the only supply of fresh air existed.

They eventually arrived at Augusta, Georgia and then to Andersonville and the prison camp. And as he continued, his story framed in my mind a picture of unbelievable suffering and depravation in the camp. He told of men barely alive wearing rags that were once their uniform. The water they existed on came from a polluted stream or puddles of rainwater. Men were dying daily as well as men pitifully waiting for death to ease them of their suffering.

And then he came to the main point of his account, the meeting up with my dear brother.

John Maltman had been experiencing the daily horrific scenes of camp life when in early July he was chosen for hospital duty. This task was considered highly by the prisoners. The prisoners assigned to the hospital had the benefit of getting out from the stench and filth of the camp to an area where there was fresh air, or at least more breathable than in the camp. Also there was a chance at better rations and with them some hope of survival. This is how he came to meet up with Harrison.

Maltman's duty for the day was to act as a stretcher bearer and help carry the infirmed from the camp to the hospital. He said that this job was not for the weak of heart for the conditions of the poor souls was usually beyond a doctor's care. As he walked by a hospital bed he heard his name called out in a weak voice. He stopped and looked at the man astride him. The patient asked, "Sergeant Maltman, have you come for me?"

He looked at the man not able to come up with a name until the patient grabbed Maltman's arm and said, "I'm Harrison McFall, Company E, and you're a face from home." Maltman told me that he was shocked when he realized who the patient was. He remembered Harrison as a young man of blue eyes and a look of youth. Here in the bed laid a man certainly not young with a pallid face and sunken, sad eyes. His weight could not have been one hundred and when he spoke it was the voice of an old man, a voice weakened from months of misery.

Maltman clasped Harrison's hands and with a smile called him by name, "Harrison McFall, how very glad we once again are together." Harrison's voice seemed to strengthen as he told Maltman his story of capture.

Harrison recalled his capture back in November 1863 as the regiment was retreating back to Knoxville. He and James Morgan were being chased by rebels as they sought shelter in an old tobacco barn. But they became surrounded and forced to surrender.

They and other Federals were led by their captors in an exhausting march and by overcrowded boxcars back east, eventually arriving in Richmond. During their journey they were robbed of everything but their shirt and pants, their shoes were highly prized by the rebels. They saw but little rations and what was given was usually a corn meal mush.

They arrived in Richmond and imprisoned at Belle Island. This camp was overcrowded as they arrived. Harrison and Morgan were put in with dozens of other Federals in an open pen no more than 20 by 20 feet. He spent most of the winter at this camp where few blankets and scarce heat was commonplace. It was at this point he became ill with chills and weakness. This ailment never left him.

The rebels began to transfer many of the men south as Belle Island became too overcrowded even for the rebels. He and Morgan were involved in a movement of a few hundred by railroad. This was in early March. His health continued to be poor as no medical care was given to anyone short of near death.

The captives eventually arrived at Andersonville and by this time Harrison could barely walk as his condition worsened with dysentery adding to his misery. He was admitted to the camp hospital about a month before Maltman saw him.

He asked about the family and Sergeant Maltman told him what he knew about the McFalls. He was very interested to hear about the regiment and its activities. Maltman told him of the fierce fighting in Virginia and how he got captured.

Harrison also asked Maltman if I had kept hold of his personal effects. The Sergeant said he believed I had, which seemed to comfort him.

Maltman then said he would try to return and talk with him again.

John Maltman continued his account.

On the morning of Wednesday, July 27th he again was present in the hospital and stopped by Harrison's bed. What he saw caused him to shudder in surprise. Harrison's face was ashen and his eyes had an icy stare. As Maltman spoke, Harrison could only respond in a faint whisper. Death was drawing near.

In a weakened voice Harrison spoke his last words, "Sergeant, when you return home please tell my family I love them dearly and we'll all meet again with our Lord."

He then said, "please fix me". I knew what he meant as I covered him with a thin sheet, I folded his hands on his chest, and sat by him until I saw his chest rise for the final time.

Maltman mentioned that Harrison faced death bravely and with dignity.

Maltman went on to continue his own story of how he escaped while being transported to another prison camp. He was eventually recaptured but was finally exchanged and returned to our regiment. And much to his surprise was given a commission and assigned to Company H.

I thanked him greatly for his information on Harrison and wished him well on his new assignment.

Needless to say I was much saddened by Maltman's account. I had tried to keep hope alive that Harrison would return though I knew the chances were small.

I knew that I had to notify the family back home which meant I would have to write the letter I dreaded the most.

I knew the family should hear the news from me before they heard from some other source so on Christmas Eve I wrote home.

Petersburg, Virginia
Saturday, December 24, 1864

Dear Parents and Sisters,

I hope this letter finds all of you in good health. I do apologize for not writing as often as I know I should. Although Company E and the regiment have not tangled with the rebels, we have still been kept on the move with a bushel full of tasks.

We are now in winter quarters which means our nearest enemy is the weather rather than the rebels. I've been sharing a first rate shelter of logs and boards rather than a drafty tent.

As you may of heard I got promoted to sergeant which means a bit more pay and a barrel full of new duties. Now, I'm more responsible for the company's condition such as appearance, health and discipline. Although our usual daily routine can be guarding prisoners or clearing trees, we do still go on picket duty and need to be alert for any rebel shenanigans.

We were able to vote in the presidential election and I'm proud to say our regiment's voice was heard loud and clear as we backed Mr. Lincoln by a one-hundred vote margin over General McClellan. Now hopefully the Democrats and their Copperhead friends will work for our cause rather than against it.

Before I go on I have some very sad news to pass on. If you remember, John Maltman was captured at the battle of Spottsylvania back in May. But miraculously he was exchanged and has this month returned to the regiment. In fact he has been promoted to Lieutenant of Company H. he made a point of looking me up and told me of Harrison's death at the rebel prison camp in Georgia.

He said Harrison died last July 27th of disease while in the prison hospital. He said he was with Harrison while he was in the camp hospital. I am told Harrison's spirit and mind were keen and alert though his body suffered. Harrison talked often of our family and hoping to see everyone again. John Maltman was in the hospital on the day Harrison died and told me Harrison's last wish was that we all know that he loved us, and his God very much.

I know this news is a shock to us all. He was a good soldier and a loving brother. Take some comfort that his pain has ended and he waits for our reunion with him.

Colonel Luce has resigned the regimental command due to poor health. He is a brave and able soldier. Lieutenant Colonel Swift takes over for him. I think he'll be a fine addition.

Spending another Christmas away from home saddens me. I can see in my mind your parlor and the festive decorations. The smells of your biscuits baking and the sight of Pa carving the Christmas goose is before me now. But, we here still have a job to do, to bring this infernal war to an end. I can't believe the rebels can struggle much longer. The prisoners we capture are a sight beyond belief. Their uniforms are mostly rags, some are barefoot and they tell of being issued rations barely enough for dogs to live on.

We deeply appreciated the food baskets sent by the Cone and the Paint Creek Assemblies.

On Christmas, Chaplain Greene will hold a service and we've been told to expect a special dinner after. I'll end now as the bugle calls for sergeants to report. I can only hope the day arrives soon when the last bugle sounds, the call that reports the end of this war. Give my best wishes to all, keep hope alive, and Merry Christmas and have comfort knowing our dear Harrison is with the Lord.

With affection Daniel,

Company E
Acting Engineers
1st Division
9th Corps
Army of the Potomac

The new year, 1865, brought a letter from home.

Paint Creek
Saturday, December 24, 1864

Dear Brother,

We here hope that as we approach Christmas, this letter finds you safe in winter quarters.

I certainly had hoped that this war would have ended by now but as long as the South follows the foolish and deadly politics of Jeff Davis, their defeat will only be more complete when it happens.

Here in Michigan, we rejoiced in President Lincoln's reelection and I read that the Seventeenth Michigan's votes showed their loyalty to him and our country.

We are thankful that you continue to perform pioneer and provost duty though I know you aint far from a "nest of bees."

The fall harvest went well. John, Thomas, and I brought in your crops with rain storm slowing us for a few days.

Lomira, the children, and I will be going tomorrow to join everyone for Christmas Sabbath. John and Emma has invited all the family to their place after for dinner. The snow hasn't been piling up so far which means we can

I Hear the Bugle's Call

still go about in the carriage and not the sleigh.

Another Christmas without you home is not what we had been looking for. We can only pray that with spring comes peace. We also continue to hold out hope for Harrison's return though, we read that prisoner exchanges aren't that common anymore. Perhaps Harrison and John Maltman, and James Masters are together and looking out for each other. We can only pray so.

Louis Haner, passes on his thanks for your letters to him. He's a good neighbor and a good Christian.

I'll be ending now as the day is ending and chores come early. And before I forget, Lomira reminded me to ask if the church ladies packages arrived?

Merry Christmas,

Schuyler, Lomira and family

As 1865 began its march as a new year, most of the men in camp began talking of the war's end coming in spring. Some who enjoyed gambling even started taking bets on which day and month peace finally arrives. I stayed away from such talk as I feared overconfidence could be proven wrong, deadly wrong.

The winter continued its skirmish with both armies through January into February. One advantage of pioneer duty was our company had first knowledge of firewood locations which we put to use often.

brother John sent a letter in February which was greatly received.

The Last Bugle Has Sounded

Paint Creek
Thursday, February 2, 1865

Dear Brother Daniel,

This letter probably comes as a surprise as it's been awhile since I've written.

As winter drags on so do the chores as you well know. We've not seen a lot of snow but the temperatures are not kind to man or beast. We haven't seen any day above 30 degrees and for the nights well, near zero is the usual. I've made sure your house has been kept up as I put a fire going in your stove whenever I'm over there.

We were all shocked and saddened about the news of Harrison's death. Of course Ma and Pa took it the hardest. Pastor Hoover led a memorial service for family and friends. Many good people attended and we all spoke of fond memories of our dear brother. The Pastor reminded us of the many good qualities of Harrison and of course his courage and devotion to our country. We'd rather not dwell on how he died and where but, that now he has found his own peace. We must go on carrying his memory with us.

Your livestock is faring well but you have lost some hens to an invading fox. Thomas and I did set a trap and snared it a few days back.

In the newspapers we're reading how the South is on its last legs. It sure would seem if Petersburg would fall so goes the rebel cause. Of course you're the expert on that kind of talk. Any hope for a last minute prisoner exchange?

Your letters to Schuyler and Ma and Pa get passed around as we all look forward to them.

Emma wants me to ask if the last box of baked goods made it to you? She and Lomira are getting another box together. Expect a box of the items you asked for coming soon.

We are relieved that your situation is relatively safe. Hopefully, the Virginia winter hasn't been too harsh to you and the others.

I'll end now and hope to read a letter from you when you have the time.

I Hear the Bugle's Call

John, Emma and family

Spring arrived with added optimism that General Lee's army could not hold out much longer. In fact, on the 25th of March the rebels tried to break our cordon around Petersburg as a battle took place near Fort Steadman. Our regiment was called into formation as a protective barrier encircling General Willcox's headquarters, the rebel breakout attempt failed with few casualties on our part.

I did have time later to write Schuyler a letter.

Petersburg, Virginia
Monday, March 27, 1865

Dear Brother Schuyler,

Well another spring has begun here in Virginia. I trust the grasp of winter is also letting up back in Michigan. When I close my eyes I can feel the warmth of the sun and hear the songbirds, its like home until I refocus on my surroundings and see men engaged in war with all the smells and clamor of an army camp. This certainly is not like home.

The regiment still occupies a place outside of Petersburg. We have had some recent action as the rebels attempted a breakout from our siege at a place called Fort Steadman. We formed a skirmish line in front of General Willcox's Headquarters and although the fight was intense, the rebels were forced back with our losses of one killed, one wounded.

As our siege of Petersburg has continued we've seen a steady flow of runaway slaves who braved capture to head to our lines. Some of these people tell of wild stories that their owners tried to scare them with. Some were told that we Yankees would cut off their ears, that we had devil-like horns, and boiled children for our meal. The contraband said they didn't believe such talk, but some did act in a cautious way at first meeting.

We were right pleased to hear that Mr. Lincoln has taken the oath once more.

The Last Bugle Has Sounded

He's been a brave and honest man throughout this trouble and we want to finish this war as our duty to him.

I have kept Harrison's possessions as I had the hope that one day he would return to claim them. One of the items is an interesting-looking pouch that I believe contain the letters from Miss Welch. Perhaps she would appreciate their return.

Captain Logan is our company commander since his release from prison camp. Lieutenant Warner is his adjutant.

I'm sure you and the men are busy getting ready for spring plowing. If the talk I hear holds true, I might be coming home to help. I can't see how General Lee can keep his army together much longer. I'm getting anxious for the day when the last bugle sounds. I'll write when I can.

                    Daniel,

                    Company E
                    17th Michigan Vol. Regiment
                    1st Brigade
                    1st Division
                    9th Corps
                    Army of the Potomac

On April 2nd the Army of the Potomac began its final assault on the Petersburg fortifications. And to our great surprise the rebels were pushed back and skeedaddled south. And on April 6th our regiment was ordered to enter the rebel capital of Richmond as the rebels had abandoned it. I was ordered to lead a detail of men charged with guarding a handful of military warehouses not torched by the retreating rebels. We were to keep looters or any remaining rebels away.

It was at this point when on April 9th we heard the joyous news of Lee's surrender. Captain Logan came riding into camp on a mount he had obtained a little past noon and he was yelling and carrying on. He quickly called assembly and gave us the great news. Forgetting we were at attention, voices began shouting and caps took flight in our celebration. At long last this storm of death and despair is nearing its end.

Captain Logan told us that Lee's army has surrendered, but General Johnston's force down in North Carolina still was on the loose. But for us it mattered little for we figured General Sherman and his army would quickly "hog tie" Johnston. It wouldn't be our worry.

On Sunday April 16th Lieutenant Colonel Swift called for a regimental formation before noon. We formed up thinking he might tell us when we could be heading home. But the look on his face as we formed told us this wasn't going to be good news.

The Lieutenant Colonel began, "Men, I have a very sad report to give you today. Our beloved President was shot last night in Washington and has passed this morning. A cowardly assassin by the name of Booth is suspected in this foul deed. In fact, a small gang of accomplices also attempted to murder the Vice President and Secretary of State. As of the last report, we believe they failed in those attempts."

The news given by the Lieutenant Colonel shocked all of us as if he had spoken of a dear family member's death. The company was dismissed and as we walked back to our tents voices could be heard speaking words of sympathy for the Lincoln family, and vows of revenge to the perpetrators. Who else was behind such a heinous crime? Did Jefferson Davis or General Lee have knowledge of the plot before the shot was fired?

Time, it is said, heals all wounds, and I look forward to them healing. Our country must like a wounded soldier now begin to heal, but with the murder of our great president, the recovery could be painfully slow.

Around April 24th the regiment was ordered back north to Alexandria. Before moving I wrote home to Ma and Pa.

The Last Bugle Has Sounded

                                      Richmond, Virginia
                                      April 17, 1865

Dear Parents and Sisters,

I trust everyone there has heard the great news of Lee's surrender! On April 9th, the day of the surrender to General Grant, our regiment was at Richmond as part of the Provost Guard. My duty was to be in charge of some of our Company as they watched over one of the rebels' military warehouses. Even though the fighting was over around the city, we were still on alert for looters or other troublemakers.

As you may have read, the Army of the Potomac was successful in assaulting the Petersburg defenses on April 2nd and took control of the town. The rebels then "high tailed" it south and west trying to get to the Carolinas. But our cavalry was able to cut off their escape and supplies. The rebels were forced to abandon Richmond as Jefferson Davis and what is left of the Confederate government went on the run. We then took control of the city and found much of it destroyed by the rebels.

We got wind of the surrender news when a courier rode into camp from Appomattox on the afternoon of the 9th. Lieutenant Colonel Swift, our regimental commander, called assembly and read us the news. Most of the men couldn't believe our ears at first. I and Andrew Kelly took hold of each other's shoulders and danced a jig. We then realized we were still in formation but the Captain just laughed and said, "Well now I can see that this regiment can dance as well as it fights!" With that we all had a good laugh.

Our great feeling of joy and relief came to a sudden halt when we heard the news last Saturday of the death of our President.

I can only guess that the shock of that news was as immediate at home as it was here. How unfair it is that as the end of the war comes near our great President is not allowed to enjoy the results of his determined effort and those of his soldiers. We hope that the search for the assassin Booth, and his accomplices will be successful soon.

General Sherman's forces are in pursuit of General Johnston's down in North

I Hear the Bugle's Call

Carolina. When Sherman's men bag those rebels we then can really begin to see the storm clouds disappear.

My wish is that in a short while I will be stepping off the train in Ypsilanti and seeing my family in peace at last. What a day that will be!

>With affection, Daniel
>Company E
>17th Michigan Vol Regiment
>1st Brigade
>1st Division
>9th Corps
>Army of the Potomac

And while in Alexandria anxiously awaiting any news of our muster date I received a fine letter from Schuyler.

>Paint Creek
>Friday, May 5, 1865

Dear Brother,

How great is our relief now that this ungodly war has ended. Everyone here was so happily surprised by the news of Lee's surrender. It seemed when we read the newspaper report a huge storm had lifted from overhead.

Our joy quickly became sorrow when we learned of the news of Mr. Lincoln's assassination by the coward Booth. How cruel an act, to end the life of a good and honest man when the country needs him the most as North and South must learn to get along once more.

Following the news Pastor Hoover led the congregation in a memorial service. He spoke quite well about Mr. Lincoln's belief in charity for all.

The Last Bugle Has Sounded

Now that the fighting is done we hope to hear good news from you about when you're coming home. In fact, I'm hoping you're on your way as I write this letter.

I'll end now as Lomira is calling me to dinner. Write as soon as you get word on coming home. I'll have the horses hitched and ready to head for the train station with the utmost speed.

Brother Schuyler,

One of the good events that took place while we were near Washington was our taking part in the Grand Review in May.
Early on the morning of Tuesday, May 23rd our regiment marched into Washington and stopped near the Capitol. The 17th was led by Lieutenant Colonel Swift as the Ninth Corps formed in place. General Willcox led our division as General Parke led our Corps. We marched down the street in fine shape and looked right sharp as we came in front of President Johnson, General Grant, Sherman and other dignitaries. The parade lasted most of the day as the Army of the Potomac passed in review. General Sherman's Army of the West had their moment in the sun on the following day. I wrote a letter to Schuyler describing the review and my hope for early return home.

Washington City
Wednesday, May 29, 1865

Dear Brother,

I was pleased to receive your letter of the 5th inst. I am hopeful this may be the last letter you receive from me as we all here are anxious to get going towards home.

But I can't pass on telling you what a parade we were in yesterday. The whole Army of the Potomac marched in what was called the Grand Review. On Tuesday, General Meade led the army down the street past the President's House where President Johnson, General Grant, Sherman, and others, stood as we marched by. General Parke led the Ninth Corps, and I couldn't believe the sight of so many soldiers in the march. General Willcox led our division and Lieutenant Colonel Swift leading the Seventeenth. Our brigade included the 27th Michigan, 109th New York, 37th Wisconsin, 51st Pennsylvania and the 79th New York. It took most of the morning and afternoon to march all the men. We heard the bands playing and the applause of the people lined up thick as leaves on a tree. General Sherman and the army from the west got their turn today.

The good feeling I have from the day is tempered amight when I think about the good friends we've lost since 1862 and the death of our beloved Harrison. The regiment has really no assigned duty right now and the inactivity has become a real chore. We see other regiments mustering out and heading home but we sit here.

But this sitting can't go on much longer and then we can look forward to that train ride home. How different it will be from the trip here in 62, the train us three took East when every step was a celebration. Will we feel like celebrating now?

Pass on to Ma and Pa that I'm safe and will be home soon. I'll try and surprise all.

>   Daniel,
>
>   Company E
>   17th Michigan Vol Infantry
>   1st Brigade
>   1st Division
>   Army of the Potomac

On June 2nd our regiment finally got the news we were all waiting to hear. Lieutenant Colonel Swift called us into formation and told us that on June 3rd our regiment would be officially mustered out of Federal service! How sweet the sound of those words! How long the wait to hear them.

Early on that Saturday, we formed up and after inspection our regiment marched to a place called the Delaney House. Here Lieutenant Colonel Swift read an order from the President releasing us from Federal service to be then allowed to return home to Michigan.

On Sunday the 4th of June, our regiment boarded a train going west, which would retrace our route we took so long ago in August of '62.

As I and others were carried west through the countryside of New York and Pennsylvania, I couldn't help but recall those early days when we headed east being feted at every stop as heroes though we hadn't fired a round.

Now when we stop no bands play, no flowers or cakes are offered. I guess the war's length and intensity has hardened us all to the idea of a "glorious war."

Our train reached Cleveland on June 5th and two steamers—the Morning Star and City of Cleveland awaited us. Company E was assigned the Morning Star and we set a course for Detroit.

Our final formation took place in Detroit on June 7th as General Willcox read to us the order from Governor Blair relieving us from our volunteer service.

After being paid for the final time, I bought a ticket for Ypsilanti. I had in mind a surprise appearance.

When I arrived at the depot in Ypsilanti, I had a stroke of luck as I encountered Louis Haner who was in town selling wood. When I approached him, he at first did not recognize me. I guess war does that to a person. When he did finally recognize my voice, we grasped each other warmly.

Louis agreed to give me a ride out to Paint Creek so I could surprise everyone. The trip south out of town was a most pleasant one. As I sat atop his wagon my head pivoted like a weathercock looking over the sights as we traveled those ten miles.

I asked him to drop me off a short walk from Schuyler's farm. As he did he agreed to deposit my baggage at my farmhouse on his way home.

I then walked up the road to Schuyler's path and then to the front door. As I knocked, Lomira came to the door. I responded, "would you have a bit of food for a poor soldier, madam?" She looked a bit puzzled at me then a broad smile came upon her as she opened the door and threw her arms around my shoulders. "Hallelujah, our prayers have been answered!" was her happy response. She then called out, "Young'ens come see who's here!" With that Preston and Elenora came running from the kitchen. At first they weren't too sure who I was until their mother said, "Come children, this is your Uncle Daniel finally come home!" I knelt and gave each a hug while stating "My gosh, how these lambs have grown!" Little Perry was asleep in the far room. Then I heard footsteps outside the kitchen. As I sat down at the table, in walks Schuyler and John expecting their noon meal.

I immediately rose, saluted and announced, "Company E reporting home!" I can't really describe the look on Schuyler's face as he recognized me. We hadn't seen each other since that hellish day along Antietam Creek.

I'm sure in our faces the toll of war was evident. He looked much older than I remembered and his eyes lacked the brightness of years past. I'm sure my appearance wasn't the same as he remembered either. We shook hands heartily and I in turn did the same to my dear brother John.

Lomira told us to sit as she brought dishes containing foods I had only dreamt about. She told me to fill my plate, and being a good soldier I did. The plate was soon engulfed with potatoes, biscuits, slices of beef, green beans, and a gravy to pour. I said, "Lomira, my poor stomach aint going to know what's caused this change of rations, but it will appreciate it no doubt about it."

I updated my brothers on what I knew about James Masters, John Maltman and other local men. We also discussed the tragic loss of Harrison. I also mentioned I had Harrison's personal items including a very touching letter that Harrison had received soon after being captured. I later learned its contents...

The Last Bugle Has Sounded

Cone
Thursday, December 10, 1863

Dear Harrison,

I write this letter, not really sure what to think or say. My Pa has come from the mill with fearful news. He spoke to your Pa and was told you have been declared missing from battle! He said your Pa had only slim knowledge of the details that came from Daniel.

Though I nearly fainted when I heard the news, I cannot believe this could happen. I am convinced that you were merely separated for a time and now as you read this you are sitting at your campfire with you brother and others. I refuse to think otherwise.

That being so, I'll carry on with the regular goings on here at home.

We've read about the travels of your division in Tennessee and the march to Knoxville. Everyone here continues to be proud of you and the men of the Seventeenth Michigan. The Copperheads here in Michigan continue to show their disloyalty by yelling for peace now and forgetting the sacrifice of men like you and your brothers. As my Pa says he don't give a d_ _ _ for their kind.

As Christmas is nearing, the ladies of the church are knitting socks and scarves, which together with other treasures, you and others should be receiving soon.

The weather here has certainly become winter-like as the north winds blow snowflakes on a regular turn. My Pa refers to the cold North wind as an angry wind, a wind that foretells sadness. I cannot allow myself the same feeling.

I will end this letter now with these thoughts. We have known each other since we both sat on the benches at Cone School. Our families have walked to Sabbath service together more times than I can count. I now wear a brooch that is very special to me and will be forever, a symbol of an enduring friendship. This will always be so.

I Hear the Bugle's Call

Farewell, Harrison. May God be with you.

Katie

After the meal I asked if Schuyler or John could take me over to see my parents and sisters.

Schuyler said he'd welcome the task and so we left to travel the six miles to our parents farm over near Cone.

We first stopped at my farm as we took a quick walk around. It looked pretty near like I left it and I told Schuyler that I would be beholden to him, John and Thomas for a long time for their care of the place.

We reached our parent's farm and Schuyler walked up to the door first and knocked. Ma came to the door and remarked, "Schuyler, since when you got formal, knocking on the door?" Schuyler spoke up, "Ma, I got a wayward soul here who'd like to come in and rest." With that, I came from around the corner and grabbed Ma with a huge hug. The look of surprise that I saw on her face was indescribable. It was the greeting I had been thinking about for a long time. Ma then went out the back door and began ringing the meal bell. Her intention was to fetch Pa from the barn.

Pa then came sauntering up to the door asking in his usual bellowing voice, "what's the commotion, we finished eating an hour ago?" As he enters we meet and I can once again see that grizzled, tired face. And as we embrace I notice a few tears on his cheeks.

My sisters, Mariah and Jane, then came home from helping their neighbor, Mrs. Welch with some chores. We all again embraced in a most happy reunion. I would meet up later with my other sisters, Catherine and Mary.

I spent the afternoon with my family, then Schuyler took me back to my farm. I had thought about visiting Katie Welch. I had written her when I learned the tragic news about Harrison's death. I could only imagine her sorrow as she read the sad news. I am told she comes from a strong Christian family who I trust will support her in this time of melancholy. I believe I may pay her a call when the dark clouds of grief clear away from all of us.

Before Schyler left to go home he and I sat and he talked how his experience had changed him. Since returning home he has become more thankful for the little things, such as the singing of the birds, the sound of a child's laughter, the sound of the wind through the trees rather than the shrieks of men in battle.

Schuyler said that since being home he has gotten on well but there are times, especially at night, when the battle returns, when the march begins again and he hears once again the sound of bullets on bone, like cracking walnuts.

I told him I also hope to view life differently and to welcome the small joys of peace. I said, "Brother, I know we both pray that the sacrifice our dear brother and the many other brave men gave will be worth the cost, when the last bugle calls."

I Hear the Bugle's Call

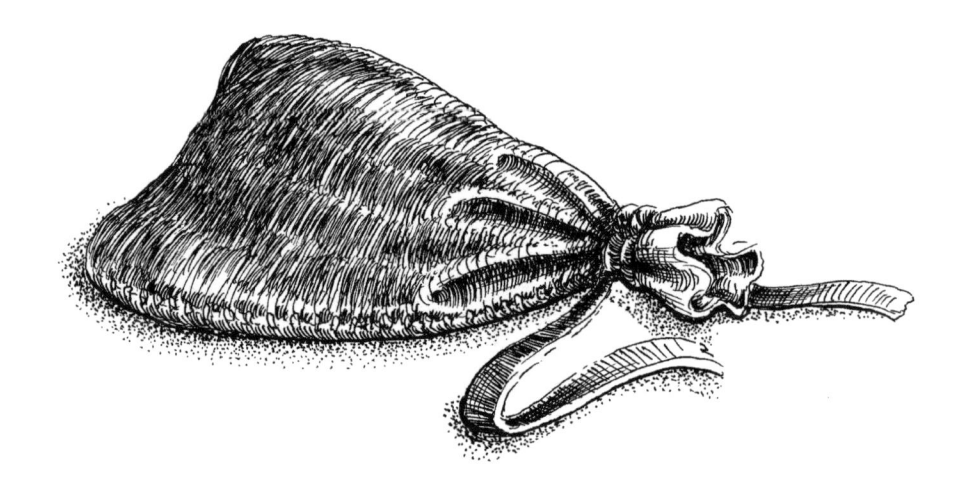

The Journey Ends

"Jacob!," "Jacob!" "What are you doing up there?" As I hear my name called out I open my eyes, and to my surprise I once again found myself sitting in the rocking chair amid piles of dusty old letters. The attic of my Great-Aunt Mildred's had become a bit darker as the sun's rays through the west window had lowered. It appeared the afternoon had gone by. As I gained some idea of where I was I yelled down, "I'm okay Mom, I'll be coming down soon!" How long have I been up here? As I looked at my watch I'd seen its been about two hours. But from what I have just gone through, it seems more like two lifetimes.

As I stacked up the letters into one pile I thought, now what would I say to my family downstairs? There's no way they'd believe the story of me living the Civil War as a real person. I had no proof. It's not exactly a believable story. So, I decided to go downstairs and just share my discovery of the cane and all the letters. Finding the treasures I did would be a giant surprise to everyone, and I should be able to put together one awesome history report. I'll have to keep my real adventure to myself, hoping I can one day somehow prove to everyone what really did take place.

When I showed everyone the letters and the cane, they were shocked at my discoveries. My Great-Aunt Mildred said, "See, I told you there would be something up there worth digging through." My Grandpa Norm couldn't be happier as I helped not only confirm what we knew about the McFall brothers but also added a whole lot more to their story.

As years passed this bizarre journey gave me a look into history that was real, which was raw, and very human as I became Daniel. As I grew to adulthood I felt at times I was living two lives, one in present time and one in the past. While walking through the neighborhood or working in the yard, a breeze would carry an unusual scent or a sound from far off in the distance which would cause me to stop as if to remind me of another place, another time.

I Hear the Bugle's Call

More than a few years had passed when my family and I were driving down to Florida for a much needed vacation. As we drove south on I-75 from Michigan we neared Atlanta, Georgia. I had a secret destination in mind and mentioned it to my wife, Jane and son, John. "Let's take a side trip before we leave the state," I proposed. Knowing my lifelong interest in history there was no doubt in their minds that this side trip must be an historical site of some kind.

We turned off I-75 at Exit 135 and headed southwest. It wasn't long before we came to the sign "Andersonville National Historic Site."

We stopped at the Visitor Center and I asked the Park Ranger where we might fine the gravesite of Harrison McFall. He quickly gave us the gravesite number and map location. As we got out of the car I asked Jane and John to stay back and let me find Harrison's grave. They look a bit puzzled and even more so as I took from the car a small draw-string bag and a hand trowel. As they held back by the car I walked twenty paces up to headstone #4078 with the name "Harrison McFall-Michigan" carved on its face. It was standing at attention in a row of at least forty others representing most of the Union states.

I approached the headstone and knelt. As I did so a strong sensation came over me. I took the trowel and I looked around to see if any Park Rangers were about. Seeing none, I began to dig a small hole at the base of the headstone. After digging a hole the size of a tin can I removed from the bag a small leather pouch. Inside the pouch contained a lock of hair bound with a faded yellow ribbon. I placed the pouch in the ground and covered up the site. I then spoke softly, "Brother, we once fought and endured the hardships of war together. Your sacrifice was greater than mine. I now return to you a gift from a young girl who you knew long ago. You once cherished this gift as I believe, you cherished her. Rest well knowing this treasure has been returned to you. Be at peace dear Harrison."

As I walk away, I stop as I hear a sound from a distant hill, "Once again, I hear the bugle's call." The journey ends.

Muster Roll

McFall Family:

Cornelius – Died December 20, 1885 – buried Azalia Cemetery, Azalia, Michigan

Catherine – Died November 30, 1871, buried Azalia Cemetery, Azalia, Michigan

Daniel – moved to Milan, Township 1866, married Nancy White 1890. Awarded Medal of Honor – 1896 for heroic action at Spottsylvania, 1864. Died November 5, 1919. Buried Rice Cemetery, Milan, Michigan.

John – continued farming. First wife Emma died November 1869. Remarried Margaret Bell, 1872. John died June 18, 1911. Believed to be buried in Azalia Cemetery, Azalia, Michigan.

Schuyler – continued farming. Died September 11, 1912. Buried in Childs Cemetery, Augusta Township, Michigan.

Lomira – spent her life by Schuyler's side—died about 1890. Buried in Childs Cemetery, Augusta Township, Michigan.

Elenora – married twice. No children.

Preston – married to Amy Asley – divorced about 1920. Four children. Died 1940.

Perry – married Louisa Legue 1892. Three children. Died 1942.

John Maltman – returned to Michigan, eventually became an early land developer in Los Angeles, California, died January 20, 1923.

James Masters – returned to Augusta, Township, was buried in Northville, Michigan.

*Denotes a character of fiction rather than fact.

***Louis Haner** – continued farming in Augusta, Township died in 1906.

***Pastor Neal Hoover** – became Pastor of York Congregational Assembly in 1870. Died in 1925.

*Thomas and Samantha Lamkin** – farmed in Paint Creek area until both succumbed to Great Flu Pandemic of 1918.

*Katie Welch** – married Pastor James Lowden 1870. First child named Harrison, who died 1918 while in battle, World War I. Katie Welch died in 1918.

Acknowledgments

This book could not have been completed without the many individuals and institutions to which I am indebted.

The following institutions provided invaluable information in the form of primary source material and individual assistance.

I began my research investigating the information at the Ypsilanti District Library, Ypsilanti, Michigan and the Milan Public Library, Milan, Michigan. These two libraries combined provided the McFall family history gleaned from their printed obituaries and the early history of Company E.

The Eastern Michigan University Archives housed in Ypsilanti, Michigan contained more detail of Company E including a roster list and newspaper articles.

The Register of Deeds' offices and the County Clerk's offices of Monroe and Washtenaw Counties were excellent sources of McFall family deeds and other legal documents.

The State Archives of Michigan at Lansing contains the military records of the 17th Michigan Volunteer Regiment including copies of official battle reports. I am also greatly indebted to the Bentley Historical Library of the University of Michigan. I spent many hours absorbed in the personal letters kept there of Irwin Shepard, Edwin Bush, and John Maltman, all of who were members of Company E and thereby intimate participants in the Company's war experiences. By reading their accounts I had a clearer picture of the war as seen by the McFalls.

Much of the military source material came from the National Archives, Military Records Division. It is amazing to me how a person one hundred fifty years after the fact can read copies of first hand accounts as if they were completed yesterday. As I read these accounts I felt I was present with the adjutant who completed them.

The National Park Service at the battlefields of Antietam, Spottsylvania, Fredericksburg, and South Mountain were extremely helpful in describing each battle and making the visitors feel they were a part of the action.

I Hear the Bugle's Call

The acknowledging of the many individuals who aided in my work begins with the two McFall family members who contributed valuable information. First, was Ron Cheever who provided the McFall family genealogy and is a descendant of the McFall family. Second, was Norm McFall, a McFall descendent who also shared family legend and lore plus Schuyler's cane that was carved in 1863 and remains in the family. Also, to Jacob Britt for allowing me to transport him on his journey

I am greatly indebted to Bill Christen who provided essential information concerning the military history of the Seventeenth Michigan Volunteer Infantry Regiment. He has also been a valuable advisor on all aspects of Civil War military life, as well as Glenna Jo Christen and her knowledge of Victorian materials and dress. The Christen's encouragement in my pursuit of this novel and their editing expertise was crucial to its completion.

The encouragement of Mr. Ken Bobicz, who as a teaching colleague and history buff was also greatly appreciated. We spent more than a few hours driving through cemeteries looking for "old dead guys."

I also greatly appreciate the professional expertise of Tom Woodruff for his vivid illustrations. His pen has added a truer life to the characters.

Tom Vranich, Bookability of Michigan/Friesens Books, has contributed his professional skill in editing the manuscript and its construction.

My appreciation is also given in memory to Miss Coda, who was present for most of the process. As pages were composed, her agreement was expressed with a wag of the tail. Sadly, her journey ended too soon.

I could never have contemplated the writing of this book without the invaluable assistance and moral support of my wife, Barb. We began by spending hours together digging through old, dusty county records. Also we spent more than a few hot summer days traipsing through battlefields trying to picture the scenes of battle. Back home, she spent untold hours at the computer with the unwelcomed task of interpreting my handwriting and creating an understandable page. Her support for this project has been essential for its completion.

My thanks finally go out to the many friends and family who have had to endure the writing updates, and plot discussions ad nauseam.